영어 원서로 읽는 고전

Animal Farm

영어 원서로 읽는 고전 Animal Farm
조지 오웰 George Orwell

펴낸곳: 북스트릿
주소: 서울시 은평구 연서로 17길 28-10 302호
원작: 조지 오웰 George Orwell
편집 및 주석: 신찬범
북커버 및 내지 디자인: 북스트릿
E-mail: invino70@gmail.com
Homepage: https://bookstreetpress.modoo.at
Blog: blog.naver.com/invino70
Fax: 0504-405-6711
초판 2022년 3월 26일

© 2022 북스트릿 BookStreet
북스트릿의 허락없는 이 책의 일부 또는 전부의 무단 복제, 전재, 발췌를 금합니다

ISBN: 979-11-90536-20-2

영어 원서로 읽는 고전
Animal Farm

George Orwell

북스트릿
BookStreet

머리말

　이 책은 영문 고전을 깊이 있게 이해하고 감상하기 위해 기획되었습니다.

　영어 원서를 읽는 데에 있어서 가장 큰 어려움 중 하나는 생소한 단어와 구 등을 매번 영어사전에서 찾아봐야 하는 번거로움입니다. 이러한 이유로 영어 원서의 독해가 쉽지 않은 것으로 인식되고 있으며, 특히 영어가 모국어가 아닌 분이나 영어를 공부하시는 분에게 어려움이 있습니다.

　이 책은 이러한 어려움을 고려하여 영어 원서를 읽는 도중에 빈번하게 영어사전을 찾아봐야 하는 번거로움을 대폭 줄였으며, 영어사전을 될 수 있는 대로 적게 참조하면서 더 수월하게 영어 원서를 읽을 수 있게 했습니다.

　이 책에는 영문 고전의 원본 텍스트가 수록되어 있습니다. 문장 해석에 중요한 숙어, 구동사, 그 외 어려운 단어와 구 들을 선택하고 강조했습니다. 이들 단어와 구를 각 페이지 왼쪽에 단락별로 정의하고 설명했습니다. 각 단어의 발음기호를 기재하여, 어휘력을 높이는 데 도움이 되게 했습니다.

　이 책이 독자분이 영문 고전을 읽는 데 의미 있는 도움이 되기를 바랍니다.

신찬범

Animal Farm

Chapter I ·· 11
Chapter II ··· 24
Chapter III ·· 36
Chapter IV ·· 47
Chapter V ··· 56
Chapter VI ·· 71
Chapter VII ··· 84
Chapter VIII ··· 101
Chapter IX ··· 121
Chapter X ·· 138

Animal Farm

Chapter I

pophole [pɑphoul / pɔphoul] n. 동물이 드나드는 작은 출입구
lurch [lə:rtʃ] v. 비틀거리다, 비틀거리며 걷다.
scullery [skʌ́ləri] n. 부엌 옆의 작은 방, 식기실
make one's way: 어떤 곳 또는 방향으로 나아가다

go out: 불이나 빛 등이 꺼지다
boar [bɔ:r] n. 수퇘지

Mr. JONES, of the Manor Farm, had locked the hen-houses for the night, but was too drunk to remember to shut the **popholes**. With the ring of light from his lantern dancing from side to side, he **lurched** across the yard, kicked off his boots at the back door, drew himself a last glass of beer from the barrel in the **scullery**, and **made his way** up to bed, where Mrs. Jones was already snoring.

As soon as the light in the bedroom **went out** there was a stirring and a fluttering all through the farm buildings. Word had gone round during the day that old Major, the prize Middle White **boar**, had had a strange dream on the previous night and wished to

barn [bɑ:rn] n.
헛간, 광
out of the way:
방해하지 않는, 걸리적거리지 않는
regard [rigá:rd] v.
주목하다, 중시하다, 존중하다

ensconce [inskáns / -skóns] v.
몸을 편히 앉히다, 안치하다
stout [staut] adj.
뚱뚱한, 살찐
benevolent [bənévələnt] adj.
호의적인, 친절한, 인정 많은
tush [tʌʃ] n.
송곳니
perch [pə:rtʃ] v.
앉다, 자리잡다
rafter [rǽftə:r, rá:ftə:r] n.
서까래, 들보
chew the cud:
되새김질 하다
hoof [hu:f, huf] n.
발굽; (발굽을 가진 동물의) 발
lest [lest] conj.
~하지 않을까(라는)

communicate it to the other animals. It had been agreed that they should all meet in the big **barn** as soon as Mr. Jones was safely **out of the way**. Old Major (so he was always called, though the name under which he had been exhibited was Willingdon Beauty) was so highly **regarded** on the farm that everyone was quite ready to lose an hour's sleep in order to hear what he had to say.

At one end of the big barn, on a sort of raised platform, Major was already **ensconced** on his bed of straw, under a lantern which hung from a beam. He was twelve years old and had lately grown rather **stout**, but he was still a majestic-looking pig, with a wise and **benevolent** appearance in spite of the fact that his **tushes** had never been cut. Before long the other animals began to arrive and make themselves comfortable after their different fashions. First came the three dogs, Bluebell, Jessie, and Pincher, and then the pigs, who settled down in the straw immediately in front of the platform. The hens **perched** themselves on the window-sills, the pigeons fluttered up to the **rafters**, the sheep and cows lay down behind the pigs and began to **chew the cud**. The two cart-horses, Boxer and Clover, came in together, walking very slowly and setting down their vast hairy **hoofs** with great care **lest** there

mare [mɛəːr] n.
암말
foal [foul] n.
(말·나귀 따위의) 새끼
hand [hænd] n.
핸드 (손바닥의 너비, 4인치 (10.16cm)); 말의 키를 재는 단위
cynical [sínikəl] adj.
냉소적인, 비꼬는
would sooner:
차라리 ~하고 싶다, ~하는 것이 낫다
paddock [pǽdək] n.
방목장
orchard [ɔ́ːrtʃərd] n.
과수원
graze [greiz] v.
(가축 등이 풀을) 뜯어먹다,

brood [bruːd] n.
한 배 병아리; (동물의) 한 배 새끼

should be some small animal concealed in the straw. Clover was a stout motherly **mare** approaching middle life, who had never quite got her figure back after her fourth **foal**. Boxer was an enormous beast, nearly eighteen **hands** high, and as strong as any two ordinary horses put together. A white stripe down his nose gave him a somewhat stupid appearance, and in fact he was not of first-rate intelligence, but he was universally respected for his steadiness of character and tremendous powers of work. After the horses came Muriel, the white goat, and Benjamin, the donkey. Benjamin was the oldest animal on the farm, and the worst tempered. He seldom talked, and when he did, it was usually to make some **cynical** remark— for instance, he would say that God had given him a tail to keep the flies off, but that he **would sooner** have had no tail and no flies. Alone among the animals on the farm he never laughed. If asked why, he would say that he saw nothing to laugh at. Nevertheless, without openly admitting it, he was devoted to Boxer; the two of them usually spent their Sundays together in the small **paddock** beyond the **orchard**, **grazing** side by side and never speaking.

  The two horses had just lain down when a **brood** of ducklings, which had lost their mother,

file [fail] v.
줄지어 행진하다
cheep [tʃi:p] v.
(병아리 따위가) 삐악삐악 울다
nestle [nés-əl] v.
편히 몸을 가누다, 아늑하게 자리잡다
trap [træp] n.
2륜 경마차
mince [mins] v.
맵시를 내며 걷다, 뽐내며 잔걸음으로 걷다
daintily [déintili] adv.
고상하게, 우미하게, 섬세하게
flirt [flə:rt] v.
펄럭펄럭 부치다, 퍼득거리다
mane [mein] n.
(사자 따위의) 갈기; (갈기 같은) 머리털
purr [pə:r] v.
(고양이가 기분 좋은 듯이) 목을 가르랑거리다

attentively [əténtivli] adv.
주의 깊게, 세심하게

comrade [kámræd, -rid / kóm-] n.
동료, 동지, 친구, 벗
pass on:
전해주다, 양도하다, 물려주다

filed into the barn, **cheeping** feebly and wandering from side to side to find some place where they would not be trodden on. Clover made a sort of wall round them with her great foreleg, and the ducklings **nestled** down inside it and promptly fell asleep. At the last moment Mollie, the foolish, pretty white mare who drew Mr. Jones's **trap**, came **mincing daintily** in, chewing at a lump of sugar. She took a place near the front and began **flirting** her white **mane**, hoping to draw attention to the red ribbons it was plaited with. Last of all came the cat, who looked round, as usual, for the warmest place, and finally squeezed herself in between Boxer and Clover; there she **purred** contentedly throughout Major's speech without listening to a word of what he was saying.

All the animals were now present except Moses, the tame raven, who slept on a perch behind the back door. When Major saw that they had all made themselves comfortable and were waiting **attentively**, he cleared his throat and began:

"**Comrades**, you have heard already about the strange dream that I had last night. But I will come to the dream later. I have something else to say first. I do not think, comrades, that I shall be with you for many months longer, and before I die, I feel it my duty to **pass on** to you such wisdom as I have acquired. I have had a long life, I have had much time for thought as I lay alone in my **stall**, and I think I may say that I understand the nature of life on this earth as well as any animal now living. It is about this that I wish to speak to you.

"Now, comrades, what is the nature of this life of ours? Let us face it: our lives are miserable, laborious, and short. We are born, we are given just so much food as will keep the breath in our bodies, and those of us who are capable of it are forced to work to the last **atom** of our strength; and the very instant that our usefulness has **come to an end** we are slaughtered with hideous cruelty. No animal in England knows the meaning of happiness or leisure after he is a year old. No animal in England is free. The life of an animal is misery and slavery: that is the plain truth.

"But is this simply part of the order of nature? Is it because this land of ours is so poor that it cannot afford a **decent** life to those who dwell upon it? No, comrades, a thousand times no! The soil of England is **fertile**, its climate is good, it is capable of affording food in **abundance** to an enormously greater number of animals than now inhabit it. This single farm of ours would support a dozen horses, twenty cows, hundreds of sheep—and all of them living

---

stall [stɔ:l] n.
마구간, 외양간, 우리

atom [ǽtəm] n.
원자; 티끌, 극소량
come to an end:
멈추다, 끝내다

"... The life of an animal is misery and slavery: that is the plain truth.

decent [díːsənt] adj.
알맞은, 어울리는, 온당한
fertile [fə́ːrtl / -tail] adj.
비옥한, 기름진, 풍작의
abundance [əbʌ́ndəns] n.
풍부, 많음, 부유

sum up:
요약하다, 간략하게 나타내다
scene [siːn] n.
(활동) 분야, 영역
overwork [óuvərwə̀ːrk] n.
과로, 과도한 노동
abolish [əbáliʃ / əbɔ́l-] v.
폐지하다, 철폐하다, 완전히 파괴하다

plough [plau] n.
쟁기
lord [lɔːrd] n.
지배자, 군주, 주인
bare [bɛər] adj.
부족한, 겨우 ~한, 겨우 ~뿐인
minimum [mínəməm] n.
최소, 최저 한도

"... Remove Man from the scene, and the root cause of hunger and overwork is abolished for ever."

in a comfort and a dignity that are now almost beyond our imagining. Why then do we continue in this miserable condition? Because nearly the whole of the produce of our labour is stolen from us by human beings. There, comrades, is the answer to all our problems. It is **summed up** in a single word—Man. Man is the only real enemy we have. Remove Man from the **scene**, and the root cause of hunger and **overwork** is **abolished** for ever.

"Man is the only creature that consumes without producing. He does not give milk, he does not lay eggs, he is too weak to pull the **plough**, he cannot run fast enough to catch rabbits. Yet he is **lord** of all the animals. He sets them to work, he gives back to them the **bare minimum** that will prevent them from starving, and the rest he keeps for himself. Our labour tills the soil, our dung fertilises it, and yet there is not one of us that owns more than his bare skin. You cows that I see before me, how many thousands of gallons of milk have you given during this last year? And what has happened to that milk which should have been breeding up sturdy calves? Every drop of it has gone down the throats of our enemies. And you hens, how many eggs have you laid in this last year, and how many of those eggs ever hatched into chickens? The rest have all gone to market to bring in money for Jones and his men. And you, Clover, where are those four foals you bore, who should have been the support and pleasure of your old age? Each was sold at a year old—you will never see one of them again. **In return** for your four **confinements** and all your labour in the fields, what have you ever had except your bare **rations** and a stall?

"And even the miserable lives we lead are not allowed to reach their natural **span**. For myself I do not **grumble**, for I am one of the lucky ones. I am twelve years old and have had over four hundred children. Such is the natural life of a pig. But no animal escapes the cruel knife **in the end**. You young porkers who are sitting in front of me, every one of you will scream your lives out at the block within a year. To that horror we all must come—cows, pigs, hens, sheep, everyone. Even the horses and the dogs have no better fate. You, Boxer, the very day that those great muscles of yours lose their power, Jones will sell you to the **knacker**, who will cut your throat and boil you down for the foxhounds. As for the dogs, when they grow old and toothless, Jones ties a brick round their necks and drowns them in the nearest pond.

"Is it not **crystal clear**, then, comrades, that

spring [spriŋ] v.
생기다, 발생하다, 일어나다
tyranny [tírəni] n.
포학, 폭정, 전제 정치
get rid of:
없애다, 내보내다, 물리치다
why [hwai] int.
(놀라움, 항의 등을 나타내는 감탄사) 아니, 물론, 당연히
body and soul:
몸과 마음을 다하여, 혼신의 힘을 기울여
overthrow [óuvərəròu] n.
타도, 전복
rebellion [ribéljən] n.
모반, 반란, 폭동
remainder [riméində:r] n.
나머지, 잔여

resolution [rèzəlú:ʃ-ən] n.
결심, 결의
falter [fɔ́:ltər] v.
비틀거리다, 주저하다
astray [əstréi] adv.
길을 잃어, 잘못하여
prosperity [prɑspérəti / prɔs-] n. 번영, 번창, 성공

uproar [ʌ́prɔ̀:r] n.
소란, 소동

all the evils of this life of ours **spring** from the **tyranny** of human beings? Only **get rid of** Man, and the produce of our labour would be our own. Almost overnight we could become rich and free. What then must we do? **Why**, work night and day, **body and soul**, for the **overthrow** of the human race! That is my message to you, comrades: **Rebellion**! I do not know when that Rebellion will come, it might be in a week or in a hundred years, but I know, as surely as I see this straw beneath my feet, that sooner or later justice will be done. Fix your eyes on that, comrades, throughout the short **remainder** of your lives! And above all, pass on this message of mine to those who come after you, so that future generations shall carry on the struggle until it is victorious.

"And remember, comrades, your **resolution** must never **falter**. No argument must lead you **astray**. Never listen when they tell you that Man and the animals have a common interest, that the **prosperity** of the one is the prosperity of the others. It is all lies. Man serves the interests of no creature except himself. And among us animals let there be perfect unity, perfect comradeship in the struggle. All men are enemies. All animals are comrades'

At this moment there was a tremendous **uproar**. While Major was speaking four large

hindquarter [háindkwɔ̀:rtər] n. (짐승의) 궁둥이와 뒷다리, 후반신
trotter [trátə:r / trɔ́tə:r] n. 동물(특히 돼지, 양)의 발

Why, work night and day, body and soul, for the overthrow of the human race! That is my message to you, comrades: Rebellion!

dissentient [disénʃiənt] n. 의견을 달리하는 사람

enmity [énməti] n. 적의, 증오
resemble [rizémb-əl] v. 닮다
vice [vais] n. 악덕, 사악, 부도덕

rats had crept out of their holes and were sitting on their **hindquarters**, listening to him. The dogs had suddenly caught sight of them, and it was only by a swift dash for their holes that the rats saved their lives. Major raised his **trotter** for silence.

"Comrades," he said, "here is a point that must be settled. The wild creatures, such as rats and rabbits—are they our friends or our enemies? Let us put it to the vote. I propose this question to the meeting: Are rats comrades?"

The vote was taken at once, and it was agreed by an overwhelming majority that rats were comrades. There were only four **dissentients**, the three dogs and the cat, who was afterwards discovered to have voted on both sides. Major continued:

"I have little more to say. I merely repeat, remember always your duty of **enmity** towards Man and all his ways. Whatever goes upon two legs is an enemy. Whatever goes upon four legs, or has wings, is a friend. And remember also that in fighting against Man, we must not come to **resemble** him. Even when you have conquered him, do not adopt his **vices**. No animal must ever live in a house, or sleep in a bed, or wear clothes, or drink alcohol, or smoke tobacco, or touch money, or engage in trade. All the habits of Man are evil. And, above all, no

tyrannize [tírənàiz] v.
학정을 행하다, 압제하다, 학대하다

sow [sau] n.
암퇘지; (곰 따위의) 암컷
tune [tju:n] n.
곡, 곡조, 멜로디
infancy [ínfənsi] n.
유아, 유년기
hoarse [hɔ:rs] adj.
쉰 목소리의, 귀에 거슬리는

"... And, above all, no animal must ever tyrannise over his own kind. Weak or strong, clever or simple, we are all brothers. No animal must ever kill any other animal. All animals are equal."

stirring [stə́:riŋ] adj.
마음을 동요시키는, 감동시키는, 고무하는

animal must ever **tyrannise** over his own kind. Weak or strong, clever or simple, we are all brothers. No animal must ever kill any other animal. All animals are equal.

"And now, comrades, I will tell you about my dream of last night. I cannot describe that dream to you. It was a dream of the earth as it will be when Man has vanished. But it reminded me of something that I had long forgotten. Many years ago, when I was a little pig, my mother and the other **sows** used to sing an old song of which they knew only the **tune** and the first three words. I had known that tune in my **infancy**, but it had long since passed out of my mind. Last night, however, it came back to me in my dream. And what is more, the words of the song also came back—words, I am certain, which were sung by the animals of long ago and have been lost to memory for generations. I will sing you that song now, comrades. I am old and my voice is **hoarse**, but when I have taught you the tune, you can sing it better for yourselves. It is called *Beasts of England* "

Old Major cleared his throat and began to sing. As he had said, his voice was hoarse, but he sang well enough, and it was a **stirring** tune, something between *Clementine* and *La Cucaracha*. The words ran:

clime [klaim] n.
나라, 지방; 풍토
hearken [háːrkən] v.
경청하다, 귀를 기울이다
tiding [taidiŋ] n.
소식, 정보, 뉴스

o'erthrown: overthrown

harness [háːrnis] n.
마구
bit [bit] n.
재갈
spur [spəːr] n.
박차

Soon or late the day is coming,
Tyrant Man shall be o'erthrown,
And the fruitful fields of
England
Shall be trod by beasts alone .

Beasts of England, beasts of Ireland,
*Beasts of every land and **clime**,*
Hearken** to my joyful **tidings
Of the golden future time.

Soon or late the day is coming,
*Tyrant Man shall be **o'erthrown**,*
And the fruitful fields of England
Shall be trod by beasts alone.

Rings shall vanish from our noses,
*And the **harness** from our back,*
***Bit** and **spur** shall rust forever,*
Cruel whips no more shall crack.

Riches more than mind can picture,
Wheat and barley, oats and hay,
Clover, beans, and mangel-wurzels
Shall be ours upon that day.

Bright will shine the fields of England,
Purer shall its waters be,
Sweeter yet shall blow its breezes
On the day that sets us free.

For that day we all must labour,
Though we die before it break;
Cows and horses, geese and turkeys,

toil [tɔil] v.
힘써 일하다, 힘들게 걷다

pick up:
배우다, 익히다, 터득하다
by heart:
암기하여
preliminary [prilímənèri / -nəri] adj.
예비의, 준비의, 임시의
low [lou] v.
(소가) 음매 울다
whine [hwain] v.
(개가) 낑낑거리다
bleat [bli:t] v.
(양·염소·송아지가) 매애울다
whinny [hwíni] v.
(말이) 히힝 울다
quack [kwæk] v.
꽥꽥 울다

*All must **toil** for freedom's sake.*

Beasts of England, beasts of Ireland,
Beasts of every land and clime,
Hearken well and spread my tidings
Of the golden future time.

The singing of this song threw the animals into the wildest excitement. Almost before Major had reached the end, they had begun singing it for themselves. Even the stupidest of them had already **picked up** the tune and a few of the words, and as for the clever ones, such as the pigs and dogs, they had the entire song **by heart** within a few minutes. And then, after a few **preliminary** tries, the whole farm burst out into *Beasts of England* in tremendous unison. The cows **lowed** it, the dogs **whined** it, the sheep **bleated** it, the horses **whinnied** it, the ducks **quacked** it. They were so delighted with the song that they sang it right through five times in succession, and might have continued singing it all night if they had not been interrupted.

Unfortunately, the uproar awoke Mr. Jones, who sprang out of bed, making sure that there was a fox in the yard. He seized the gun which always stood in a corner of his bedroom, and let fly a charge of number 6 shot into the

pellet [pélit] n.
탄알, 산탄
perch [pə:rtʃ] n.
(새의) 횃대

darkness. The **pellets** buried themselves in the wall of the barn and the meeting broke up hurriedly. Everyone fled to his own sleeping-place. The birds jumped on to their **perches**, the animals settled down in the straw, and the whole farm was asleep in a moment.

..., the whole farm burst out into *Beasts of England* in tremendous unison. The cows lowed it, the dogs whined it, the sheep bleated it, the horses whinnied it, the ducks quacked it.

Chapter II

Three nights later old Major died peacefully in his sleep. His body was buried at the foot of the orchard.

This was early in March. During the next three months there was much secret activity. Major's speech had given to the more intelligent animals on the farm a completely new **outlook** on life. They did not know when the Rebellion predicted by Major would **take place**, they had no reason for thinking that it would be within their own lifetime, but they saw clearly that it was their duty to prepare for it. The work of teaching and organising the others fell naturally upon the pigs, who were generally recognised as being the cleverest of the animals.

lookout [lúkàut] n.
견해, 시야
take place:
발생하다, 일어나다

preeminent [priémənənt] adj.
우수한, 발군의, 탁월한
boar [bɔːr] n.
수퇘지
get one's own way:
독자적인 길을 가다, 소신대로 행동하다
vivacious [vivéiʃəs, vai-] adj.
쾌활한, 활발한, 명랑한
inventive [invéntiv] adj.
발명의, 창작의 재능이 있는, 창의력이 풍부한
nimble [nímb-əl] adj.
재빠른, 민첩한
persuasive [pərswéisiv] adj.
설득 잘하는, 설득력 있는, 구변이 좋은

elaborate [ilǽbərèit] v.
정성들여 만들다, 힘들여 고치다
expound [ikspáund] v.
설명하다
apathy [ǽpəθi] n.
냉담, 무관심, 무감동
loyalty [lɔ́iəlti] n.
충의, 충성, 성실

Pre-eminent among the pigs were two young **boars** named Snowball and Napoleon, whom Mr. Jones was breeding up for sale. Napoleon was a large, rather fierce-looking Berkshire boar, the only Berkshire on the farm, not much of a talker, but with a reputation for **getting his own way**. Snowball was a more **vivacious** pig than Napoleon, quicker in speech and more **inventive**, but was not considered to have the same depth of character. All the other male pigs on the farm were porkers. The best known among them was a small fat pig named Squealer, with very round cheeks, twinkling eyes, **nimble** movements, and a shrill voice. He was a brilliant talker, and when he was arguing some difficult point he had a way of skipping from side to side and whisking his tail which was somehow very **persuasive**. The others said of Squealer that he could turn black into white.

These three had **elaborated** old Major's teachings into a complete system of thought, to which they gave the name of Animalism. Several nights a week, after Mr. Jones was asleep, they-held secret meetings in the barn and **expounded** the principles of Animalism to the others. At the beginning they met with much stupidity and **apathy**. Some of the animals talked of the duty of **loyalty** to Mr. Jones, whom they referred to as "Master," or made

contrary [kántreri / kɔ́n-] adj.
반대의, ~에 반하는, 적합치 않은

devoted [divóutid] adj.
충실한, 헌신하는, 몰두하는
slavery [sléivəri] n.
노예 상태, 노예의 신분

counteract [kàuntərǽkt] v.
방해하다, 대항하다, 좌절시키다
talebearer [téilbɛ̀-ərə:r] n.
나쁜 소문을 퍼뜨리는 사람, 고자쟁이

elementary remarks such as "Mr. Jones feeds us. If he were gone, we should starve to death." Others asked such questions as "Why should we care what happens after we are dead?" or "If this Rebellion is to happen anyway, what difference does it make whether we work for it or not?", and the pigs had great difficulty in making them see that this was **contrary** to the spirit of Animalism. The stupidest questions of all were asked by Mollie, the white mare. The very first question she asked Snowball was: "Will there still be sugar after the Rebellion?"

"No," said Snowball firmly. "We have no means of making sugar on this farm. Besides, you do not need sugar. You will have all the oats and hay you want."

"And shall I still be allowed to wear ribbons in my mane?" asked Mollie.

"Comrade," said Snowball, "those ribbons that you are so **devoted** to are the badge of **slavery**. Can you not understand that liberty is worth more than ribbons?"

Mollie agreed, but she did not sound very convinced.

The pigs had an even harder struggle to **counteract** the lies put about by Moses, the tame raven. Moses, who was Mr. Jones's especial pet, was a spy and a **talebearer**, but he was also a clever talker. He claimed to know of the existence of a mysterious country called Sugarcandy Mountain, to which all animals went when they died. It was situated somewhere up in the sky, a little distance beyond the clouds, Moses said. In Sugarcandy Mountain it was Sunday seven days a week, clover was in season all the year round, and lump sugar and linseed cake grew on the hedges. The animals hated Moses because he told tales and did no work, but some of them believed in Sugarcandy Mountain, and the pigs had to argue very hard to persuade them that there was no such place.

Their most faithful **disciples** were the two **cart-horses**, Boxer and Clover. These two had great difficulty in thinking anything out for themselves, but having once accepted the pigs as their teachers, they absorbed everything that they were told, and passed it on to the other animals by simple arguments. They were **unfailing** in their attendance at the secret meetings in the barn, and led the singing of *Beasts of England*, with which the meetings always ended.

Now, as it turned out, the Rebellion was achieved much earlier and more easily than anyone had expected. In past years Mr. Jones, although a hard master, had been a capable farmer, but of late he had fallen on evil days.

---

disciple [disáipəl] n.
제자, 문하생, 신봉자
cart horse:
짐마차 말
unfailing [ʌnféiliŋ] adj.
신뢰할 만한, 틀림없는, 확실한

dishearten [dishá:rtn] v.
낙담시키다, 용기를 잃게 하다, 실망케 하다
take to:
습관이 되다, 좋아하게 되다
lounge [laundʒ] v.
빈둥거리다, 느긋이 기대다
underfeed [ʌ̀ndərfíːd] v.
충분한 음식을 주지 않다

rabbit [rǽbit] v.
토끼 사냥을 하다
lash [læʃ] v.
채찍질하다, 매질하다

He had become much **disheartened** after losing money in a lawsuit, and had **taken to** drinking more than was good for him. For whole days at a time he would **lounge** in his Windsor chair in the kitchen, reading the newspapers, drinking, and occasionally feeding Moses on crusts of bread soaked in beer. His men were idle and dishonest, the fields were full of weeds, the buildings wanted roofing, the hedges were neglected, and the animals were **underfed**.

June came and the hay was almost ready for cutting. On Midsummer's Eve, which was a Saturday, Mr. Jones went into Willingdon and got so drunk at the Red Lion that he did not come back till midday on Sunday. The men had milked the cows in the early morning and then had gone out **rabbiting**, without bothering to feed the animals. When Mr. Jones got back he immediately went to sleep on the drawing room sofa with the *News of the World* over his face, so that when evening came, the animals were still unfed. At last they could stand it no longer. One of the cows broke in the door of the store-shed with her horn and all the animals began to help themselves from the bins. It was just then that Mr. Jones woke up. The next moment he and his four men were in the store-shed with whips in their hands, **lashing** out in all directions. This was more than the hungry

with one accord:
하나같이, 일제히
tormentor [tɔ:rméntə:r] n.
괴롭히는 사람 또는 사물
uprising [ʌ́pràiziŋ] n.
반란, 폭동
thrash [θræʃ] v.
때리다
maltreat [mæltrí:t] vt.
학대하다, 혹사하다
frighten somebody out of their wits:
매우 놀라게 하다
give up:
그만두다, 포기하다
take to (one's) heels:
도망치다

perch [pə:rtʃ] n.
(새의) 횃대
croak [krouk] v.
(까마귀, 개구리 등이) 울다
expel [ikspél] v.
쫓아내다, 물리치다, 추방하다

animals could bear. **With one accord**, though nothing of the kind had been planned beforehand, they flung themselves upon their **tormentors**. Jones and his men suddenly found themselves being butted and kicked from all sides. The situation was quite out of their control. They had never seen animals behave like this before, and this sudden **uprising** of creatures whom they were used to **thrashing** and **maltreating** just as they chose, **frightened them** almost **out of their wits**. After only a moment or two they **gave up** trying to defend themselves and **took to their heels**. A minute later all five of them were in full flight down the cart-track that led to the main road, with the animals pursuing them in triumph.

Mrs. Jones looked out of the bedroom window, saw what was happening, hurriedly flung a few possessions into a carpet bag, and slipped out of the farm by another way. Moses sprang off his **perch** and flapped after her, **croaking** loudly. Meanwhile the animals had chased Jones and his men out on to the road and slammed the five-barred gate behind them. And so, almost before they knew what was happening, the Rebellion had been successfully carried through: Jones was **expelled**, and the Manor Farm was theirs.

For the first few minutes the animals could

gallop [gǽləp] v.
질주하다, 빠르게 뛰다
in a body:
다 같이, 한 떼로
as if / as though:
마치 ~인 것처럼
reign [rein] n.
치세, 통치, 지배
halter [hɔ́:ltər] n.
(말의) 고삐, 굴레
blinker [blíŋkər] n.
(말의) 곁눈가리개
nosebag [nóuzbæ̀g] n.
(말의 목에 거는) 꼴망태
caper [kéipər] v.
뛰어돌아다니다, 깡충거리다

All the animals capered with joy when they saw the whips going up in flames.

hardly believe in their good fortune. Their first act was to **gallop in a body** right round the boundaries of the farm, **as though** to make quite sure that no human being was hiding anywhere upon it; then they raced back to the farm buildings to wipe out the last traces of Jones's hated **reign**. The harness-room at the end of the stables was broken open; the bits, the nose-rings, the dog-chains, the cruel knives with which Mr. Jones had been used to castrate the pigs and lambs, were all flung down the well. The reins, the **halters**, the **blinkers**, the degrading **nosebags**, were thrown on to the rubbish fire which was burning in the yard. So were the whips. All the animals **capered** with joy when they saw the whips going up in flames. Snowball also threw on to the fire the ribbons with which the horses' manes and tails had usually been decorated on market days.

"Ribbons," he said, "should be considered as clothes, which are the mark of a human being. All animals should go naked."

When Boxer heard this he fetched the small straw hat which he wore in summer to keep the flies out of his ears, and flung it on to the fire with the rest.

In a very little while the animals had destroyed everything that reminded them of Mr. Jones. Napoleon then led them back to the store-shed and served out a double ration of corn to everybody, with two biscuits for each dog. Then they sang *Beasts of England* from end to end seven times running, and after that they settled down for the night and slept as they had never slept before.

But they woke at dawn as usual, and suddenly remembering the glorious thing that had happened, they all raced out into the **pasture** together. A little way down the pasture there was a **knoll** that **commanded** a view of most of the farm. The animals rushed to the top of it and gazed round them in the clear morning light. Yes, it was theirs—everything that they could see was theirs! In the ecstasy of that thought they **gambolled** round and round, they hurled themselves into the air in great leaps of excitement. They rolled in the dew, they cropped mouthfuls of the sweet summer grass, they kicked up **clods** of the black earth and **snuffed** its rich scent. Then they made a tour of inspection of the whole farm and surveyed with speechless admiration the **ploughland**, the **hayfield**, the orchard, the pool, the **spinney**. It was as though they had never seen these things before, and even now they could hardly believe that it was all their own.

Then they filed back to the farm buildings and halted in silence outside the door of the

---

pasture [pǽstʃər, pá:s-] n.
목초지, 목장
knoll [noul] n.
작은 언덕
command [kəmǽnd, -má:nd] v.
(경치가) 너려다보이다
gambol [gǽmbəl] v.
뛰놀다, 장난하다
clod [klɑd / klɔd] n.
흙덩어리, 흙
snuff [snʌf] v.
코로 들이쉬다, 냄새를 맡다
plowland/ploughland [-lǽnd]
n. 경작지, 논밭
hayfield [héifi:ld] n.
건초밭, (건초용) 풀밭
spinney [spíni] n.
덤불, 잡목숲

tiptoe [típtòu] v.
발끝으로 걷다(서다)
reproach [ripróutʃ] v.
나무라다, 책망하다, 비난하다
scullery [skʌ́ləri] n.
부엌 옆의 작은 방, 식기실
stave in:
꿰뚫어 부수다
unanimous [ju:nǽnəməs] adj.
같은 의견인, 만장일치인
resolution [rèzəlú:ʃ-ən] n.
결의; 결의안
on the spot:
그 자리에서, 즉석에서

farmhouse. That was theirs too, but they were frightened to go inside. After a moment, however, Snowball and Napoleon butted the door open with their shoulders and the animals entered in single file, walking with the utmost care for fear of disturbing anything. They **tiptoed** from room to room, afraid to speak above a whisper and gazing with a kind of awe at the unbelievable luxury, at the beds with their feather mattresses, the looking-glasses, the horsehair sofa, the Brussels carpet, the lithograph of Queen Victoria over the drawing-room mantelpiece. They were just coming down the stairs when Mollie was discovered to be missing. Going back, the others found that she had remained behind in the best bedroom. She had taken a piece of blue ribbon from Mrs. Jones's dressing-table, and was holding it against her shoulder and admiring herself in the glass in a very foolish manner. The others **reproached** her sharply, and they went outside. Some hams hanging in the kitchen were taken out for burial, and the barrel of beer in the **scullery** was **stove in** with a kick from Boxer's hoof, otherwise nothing in the house was touched. A **unanimous resolution** was passed **on the spot** that the farmhouse should be preserved as a museum. All were agreed that no animal must ever live there.

The animals had their breakfast, and then Snowball and Napoleon called them together again.

"Comrades," said Snowball, "it is half-past six and we have a long day before us. Today we begin the hay harvest. But there is another matter that must be **attended** to first."

The pigs now revealed that during the past three months they had taught themselves to read and write from an old spelling book which had belonged to Mr. Jones's children and which had been thrown on the rubbish heap. Napoleon sent for pots of black and white paint and led the way down to the five-barred gate that gave on to the main road. Then Snowball (for it was Snowball who was best at writing) took a brush between the two knuckles of his **trotter**, **painted out** MANOR FARM from the top bar of the gate and in its place painted ANIMAL FARM. This was to be the name of the farm from now onwards. After this they went back to the farm buildings, where Snowball and Napoleon sent for a ladder which they caused to be set against the end wall of the big barn. They explained that by their studies of the past three months the pigs had succeeded in reducing the principles of Animalism to Seven **Commandments**. These Seven Commandments would now be **inscribed** on the wall; they would form an

unalterable law by which all the animals on Animal Farm must live for ever after. With some difficulty (for it is not easy for a pig to balance himself on a ladder) Snowball climbed up and set to work, with Squealer a few **rungs** below him holding the paint-pot. The Commandments were written on the tarred wall in great white letters that could be read thirty yards away. They ran thus:

THE SEVEN COMMANDMENTS
1. *Whatever goes upon two legs is an enemy.*
2. *Whatever goes upon four legs, or has wings, is a friend.*
3. *No animal shall wear clothes.*
4. *No animal shall sleep in a bed.*
5. *No animal shall drink alcohol.*
6. *No animal shall kill any other animal.*
7. *All animals are equal.*

It was very neatly written, and except that "friend" was written "freind" and one of the "S's" was the wrong way round, the spelling was correct all the way through. Snowball read it aloud for the benefit of the others. All the animals nodded in complete agreement, and the cleverer ones at once began to learn the Commandments **by heart**.

"Now, comrades," cried Snowball, throwing

a point of honor:
명예에 관한 일, 체면에 관한 일
get in:
거두어들이다, 모으다

mash [mæʃ] n.
곡식알, 밀기울 등을 더운 물에 걸쭉하게 푼 가축 사료

troop [tru:p] v.
한 무리가 되어 나아가다, 떼 지어 몰려오다(가다)

down the paint-brush, "to the hayfield! Let us make it **a point of honour** to **get in** the harvest more quickly than Jones and his men could do."

But at this moment the three cows, who had seemed uneasy for some time past, set up a loud lowing. They had not been milked for twenty-four hours, and their udders were almost bursting. After a little thought, the pigs sent for buckets and milked the cows fairly successfully, their trotters being well adapted to this task. Soon there were five buckets of frothing creamy milk at which many of the animals looked with considerable interest.

"What is going to happen to all that milk?" said someone.

"Jones used sometimes to mix some of it in our **mash**," said one of the hens.

"Never mind the milk, comrades!" cried Napoleon, placing himself in front of the buckets. "That will be attended to. The harvest is more important. Comrade Snowball will lead the way. I shall follow in a few minutes. Forward, comrades! The hay is waiting."

So the animals **trooped** down to the hayfield to begin the harvest, and when they came back in the evening it was noticed that the milk had disappeared.

Chapter III

toil [tɔil] v.
힘써 일하다, 힘들게 걷다

How they **toiled** and sweated to get the hay in! But their efforts were rewarded, for the harvest was an even bigger success than they had hoped.

implement [ímpləmənt] n.
도구, 기구
drawback [drɔ́:bæ̀k] n.
결점, 약점
hind [haind] adj.
뒤의, 뒤쪽의, 후방의
mowing [móuiŋ] n.
풀베기

Sometimes the work was hard; the **implements** had been designed for human beings and not for animals, and it was a great **drawback** that no animal was able to use any tool that involved standing on his **hind** legs. But the pigs were so clever that they could think of a way round every difficulty. As for the horses, they knew every inch of the field, and in fact understood the business of **mowing** and raking far better than Jones and his men had ever done. The pigs did not actually work, but

supervise [súːpərvàiz] v.
관리하다, 감독하다, 지휘하다
assume [əsjúːm] v.
(태도, 임무, 책임 따위를) 취하다, 떠맡다
harness [háːrnis] v.
~에 마구를 채우다, 마구를 달다
to and fro:
앞뒤로, 이리저리
wisp [wisp] n.
한 조각, 한 줄기
wastage [wéistidʒ] n.
소모, 낭비
stalk [stɔːk] n.
(보리, 벼 따위의) 줄기

like clockwork:
정확히, 순조롭게
dole [doul] v.
주다, 베풀다
grudging [grʌ́dʒiŋ] adj.
인색한, 마지못해 하는
parasitical [pæ̀rəsítikəl] adj.
기생하는, 기생적인

directed and **supervised** the others. With their superior knowledge it was natural that they should **assume** the leadership. Boxer and Clover would **harness** themselves to the cutter or the horse-rake (no bits or reins were needed in these days, of course) and tramp steadily round and round the field with a pig walking behind and calling out "Gee up, comrade !" or "Whoa back, comrade!" as the case might be. And every animal down to the humblest worked at turning the hay and gathering it. Even the ducks and hens toiled **to and fro** all day in the sun, carrying tiny **wisps** of hay in their beaks. In the end they finished the harvest in two days' less time than it had usually taken Jones and his men. Moreover, it was the biggest harvest that the farm had ever seen. There was no **wastage** whatever; the hens and ducks with their sharp eyes had gathered up the very last **stalk**. And not an animal on the farm had stolen so much as a mouthful.

All through that summer the work of the farm went **like clockwork**. The animals were happy as they had never conceived it possible to be. Every mouthful of food was an acute positive pleasure, now that it was truly their own food, produced by themselves and for themselves, not **doled** out to them by a **grudging** master. With the worthless **parasitical**

inexperienced [ìnikspíəriənst] adj.
경험이 없는, 미숙한
tread out:
밟아서 짜다, 밟아서 탈곡하다
chaff [tʃæf / tʃɑ:f] n.
왕겨, 여물
pull through:
(난국, 병 등을) 헤쳐 나가다
mighty [máiti] adj.
힘이 있는, 강력한
arrangement [əréindʒmənt] n.
준비, 계획, 조정, 협정
cockerel [kákərəl / kɔ́k-] n.
어린 수탉
setback [sétbæk] n.
방해, 좌절, 차질
motto [mátou / mɔ́utou] n.
모토, 표어, 좌우명

His answer to every problem, every setback, was "I will work harder!"

human beings gone, there was more for everyone to eat. There was more leisure too, **inexperienced** though the animals were. They met with many difficulties—for instance, later in the year, when they harvested the corn, they had to **tread** it **out** in the ancient style and blow away the **chaff** with their breath, since the farm possessed no threshing machine—but the pigs with their cleverness and Boxer with his tremendous muscles always **pulled** them **through**. Boxer was the admiration of everybody. He had been a hard worker even in Jones's time, but now he seemed more like three horses than one; there were days when the entire work of the farm seemed to rest upon his **mighty** shoulders. From morning to night he was pushing and pulling, always at the spot where the work was hardest. He had made an **arrangement** with one of the **cockerels** to call him in the mornings half an hour earlier than anyone else, and would put in some volunteer labour at whatever seemed to be most needed, before the regular day's work began. His answer to every problem, every **setback**, was "I will work harder!"—which he had adopted as his personal **motto**.

But everyone worked according to his capacity. The hens and ducks, for instance, saved five bushels of corn at the harvest by gathering

stray [strei] adj.
뿔뿔이 흩어진, 산란한
grumble [grʌ́mbəl] v.
투덜대다
shirk [ʃəːrk] v.
회피하다, 기피하다, 책임을 피하다
good at:
잘하는, 능숙한, 성공적인
on the ground of(that)~:
~을 이유로, ~ 때문에, ~을 핑계로
on end:
계속해서, 끊임없이
purr [pəːr] v.
(고양이가 기분 좋은 듯이) 목을 가르랑거리다
obstinate [ábstənit / ɔ́b-] adj.
완고한, 외고집의
cryptic [kríptik] adj.
숨은, 비밀의

up the **stray** grains. Nobody stole, nobody **grumbled** over his rations, the quarrelling and biting and jealousy which had been normal features of life in the old days had almost disappeared. Nobody **shirked**—or almost nobody. Mollie, it was true, was not **good at** getting up in the mornings, and had a way of leaving work early **on the ground that** there was a stone in her hoof. And the behaviour of the cat was somewhat peculiar. It was soon noticed that when there was work to be done the cat could never be found. She would vanish for hours **on end**, and then reappear at meal-times, or in the evening after work was over, as though nothing had happened. But she always made such excellent excuses, and **purred** so affectionately, that it was impossible not to believe in her good intentions. Old Benjamin, the donkey, seemed quite unchanged since the Rebellion. He did his work in the same slow **obstinate** way as he had done it in Jones's time, never shirking and never volunteering for extra work either. About the Rebellion and its results he would express no opinion. When asked whether he was not happier now that Jones was gone, he would say only "Donkeys live a long time. None of you has ever seen a dead donkey' and the others had to be content with this **cryptic** answer.

flagstaff [flǽgstæf, flǽgstɑːf]
n. 깃대, 국기 게양대
signify [sígnəfài] v.
의미하다, 뜻하다
resolution [rèzəlúːʃ-ən] n.
결의; 결의안
put forward:
내다, 제출하다, 제안하다
by far:
매우, 몹시, 훨씬
count on:
믿다, 기대하다, 생각하다
set aside:
(돈이나 물건 등을) 따로 떼어 놓다, 모아두다
paddock [pǽdək] n.
방목장

The flag was green, Snowball explained, to represent the green fields of England, while the hoof and horn signified the future Republic of the Animals …

On Sundays there was no work. Breakfast was an hour later than usual, and after breakfast there was a ceremony which was observed every week without fail. First came the hoisting of the flag. Snowball had found in the harness-room an old green tablecloth of Mrs. Jones's and had painted on it a hoof and a horn in white. This was run up the **flagstaff** in the farmhouse garden every Sunday morning. The flag was green, Snowball explained, to represent the green fields of England, while the hoof and horn **signified** the future Republic of the Animals which would arise when the human race had been finally overthrown. After the hoisting of the flag all the animals trooped into the big barn for a general assembly which was known as the Meeting. Here the work of the coming week was planned out and **resolutions** were **put forward** and debated. It was always the pigs who put forward the resolutions. The other animals understood how to vote, but could never think of any resolutions of their own. Snowball and Napoleon were **by far** the most active in the debates. But it was noticed that these two were never in agreement: whatever suggestion either of them made, the other could be **counted on** to oppose it. Even when it was resolved—a thing no one could object to in itself—to **set aside** the small **paddock** behind the orchard as a home of rest for animals who were past work, there was a stormy debate over the correct retiring age for each class of animal. The Meeting always ended with the singing of *Beasts of England*, and the afternoon was given up to recreation.

The pigs had set aside the harness-room as a headquarters for themselves. Here, in the evenings, they studied blacksmithing, carpentering, and other necessary arts from books which they had brought out of the farmhouse. Snowball also busied himself with organising the other animals into what he called Animal Committees. He was **indefatigable** at this. He formed the Egg Production Committee for the hens, the Clean Tails League for the cows, the Wild Comrades' Re-education Committee (the object of this was to tame the rats and rabbits), the Whiter Wool Movement for the sheep, and various others, besides **instituting** classes in reading and writing. On the whole, these projects were a failure. The attempt to tame the wild creatures, for instance, broke down almost immediately. They continued to behave very much as before, and when treated with **generosity**, simply **took advantage of** it. The cat joined the Re-education Committee and was very active in it for some days. She was seen one day sitting on a roof and talking to some

---

Snowball and Napoleon were by far the most active in the debates. But it was noticed that these two were never in agreement

indefatigable [ìndifǽtigəbəl] adj. 지칠 줄 모르는, 끈기있는
institute [ínstətjùːt] v. (제도, 습관 등을) 만들다, 설치하다
generosity [dʒènərásəti / -rɔ́s-] n. 관대, 아량, 친절
take advantage of ~: ~을 최대한 활용하다

sparrows who were just out of her reach. She was telling them that all animals were now comrades and that any sparrow who chose could come and perch on her paw; but the sparrows kept their distance.

The reading and writing classes, however, were a great success. By the autumn almost every animal on the farm was **literate** in some degree.

As for the pigs, they could already read and write perfectly. The dogs learned to read fairly well, but were not interested in reading anything except the Seven Commandments. Muriel, the goat, could read somewhat better than the dogs, and sometimes used to read to the others in the evenings from scraps of newspaper which she found on the rubbish heap. Benjamin could read as well as any pig, but never exercised his **faculty**. So far as he knew, he said, there was nothing worth reading. Clover learnt the whole alphabet, but could not put words together. Boxer could not get beyond the letter D. He would trace out A, B, C, D, in the dust with his great hoof, and then would stand staring at the letters with his ears back, sometimes shaking his **forelock**, trying with all his might to remember what came next and never succeeding. On several occasions, indeed, he did learn E, F, G, H, but by the time he knew them,

---

literate [lítərit] adj.
읽고 쓸 수 있는, 학식이 있는

faculty [fǽkəlti] n.
능력, 기능, 재능

forelock [fɔ́:rlɑ̀k / -lɔ̀k] n.
앞머리, (특히 말의) 이마 갈기

content [kəntént] adj.
만족하는, 불평이 없는

maxim [mǽksim] n.
격언, 금언, 좌우명
namely [néimli] adv.
즉, 다시 말하자면

propulsion [prəpʌ́lʃən] n.
추진(력)
manipulation [mənìp-jəléiʃən] n.
손으로 다루기, 교묘한 조작
mischief [místʃif] n.
손해, 위해, 재해

it was always discovered that he had forgotten A, B, C, and D. Finally he decided to be **content** with the first four letters, and used to write them out once or twice every day to refresh his memory. Mollie refused to learn any but the six letters which spelt her own name. She would form these very neatly out of pieces of twig, and would then decorate them with a flower or two and walk round them admiring them.

None of the other animals on the farm could get further than the letter A. It was also found that the stupider animals, such as the sheep, hens, and ducks, were unable to learn the Seven Commandments by heart. After much thought Snowball declared that the Seven Commandments could in effect be reduced to a single **maxim**, **namely**: "Four legs good, two legs bad." This, he said, contained the essential principle of Animalism. Whoever had thoroughly grasped it would be safe from human influences. The birds at first objected, since it seemed to them that they also had two legs, but Snowball proved to them that this was not so.

"A bird's wing, comrades," he said, "is an organ of **propulsion** and not of **manipulation**. It should therefore be regarded as a leg. The distinguishing mark of Man is the *hand*, the instrument with which he does all his **mischief**."

The birds did not understand Snowball's long words, but they accepted his explanation, and all the humbler animals set to work to learn the new maxim **by heart**. FOUR LEGS GOOD, TWO LEGS BAD, was inscribed on the end wall of the barn, above the Seven Commandments and in bigger letters. When they had once got it by heart, the sheep developed a great liking for this maxim, and often as they lay in the field they would all start **bleating** "Four legs good, two legs bad! Four legs good, two legs bad!" and keep it up for hours on end, never growing tired of it.

Napoleon took no interest in Snowball's committees. He said that the education of the young was more important than anything that could be done for those who were already grown up. It happened that Jessie and Bluebell had both **whelped** soon after the hay harvest, giving birth between them to nine sturdy puppies. As soon as they were weaned, Napoleon took them away from their mothers, saying that he would make himself responsible for their education. He took them up into a **loft** which could only be reached by a ladder from the harness-room, and there kept them in such **seclusion** that the rest of the farm soon forgot their existence.

The mystery of where the milk went to was soon cleared up. It was mixed every day into

mash [mæʃ] n.
곡식알, 밀기울 등을 더운 물에 걸쭉하게 푼 가축 사료
windfall [wíndfɔ̀ːl] n.
바람에 떨어진 과실; 예기치 않았던 횡재
assume [əsjúːm] v.
~을 당연한 것으로 여기다, 가정하다
as a matter of course:
물론, 당연히
murmur [mə́ːrmər] v.
낮게 속삭이다, 중얼거리다, 불평을 하다

selfishness [sélfiʃnis] n.
이기주의
privilege [prívəlidʒ] n.
특권, 특전
brainworker [bréinwə̀ːrkər] n.
정신 노동자
welfare [wélfɛ̀ər] n.
복지, 후생
for one's sake, for the sake of ~:
을 위하여, ~을 생각해서

the pigs' **mash**. The early apples were now ripening, and the grass of the orchard was littered with **windfalls**. The animals had **assumed as a matter of course** that these would be shared out equally; one day, however, the order went forth that all the windfalls were to be collected and brought to the harness-room for the use of the pigs. At this some of the other animals **murmured**, but it was no use. All the pigs were in full agreement on this point, even Snowball and Napoleon. Squealer was sent to make the necessary explanations to the others.

"Comrades!" he cried. "You do not imagine, I hope, that we pigs are doing this in a spirit of **selfishness** and **privilege**? Many of us actually dislike milk and apples. I dislike them myself. Our sole object in taking these things is to preserve our health. Milk and apples (this has been proved by Science, comrades) contain substances absolutely necessary to the well-being of a pig. We pigs are **brainworkers**. The whole management and organisation of this farm depend on us. Day and night we are watching over your **welfare**. It is **for *your* sake** that we drink that milk and eat those apples. Do you know what would happen if we pigs failed in our duty? Jones would come back! Yes, Jones would come back! Surely, comrades," cried

whisk [hwisk] v.
재빨리 움직이다, 흔들다

light [lait] n.
관점, 견해, 양상
obvious [ábviəs / ɔ́b-] adj.
분명한, 명백한, 명확한

Squealer almost pleadingly, skipping from side to side and **whisking** his tail, "surely there is no one among you who wants to see Jones come back?"

Now if there was one thing that the animals were completely certain of, it was that they did not want Jones back. When it was put to them in this **light**, they had no more to say. The importance of keeping the pigs in good health was all too **obvious**. So it was agreed without further argument that the milk and the windfall apples (and also the main crop of apples when they ripened) should be reserved for the pigs alone.

"... We pigs are brainworkers. The whole management and organisation of this farm depend on us.

Chapter IV

mingle [míŋgəl] v.
섞이다, 사귀다, 어울리다

By the late summer the news of what had happened 'on Animal Farm had spread across half the county. Every day Snowball and Napoleon sent out flights of pigeons whose instructions were to **mingle** with the animals on neighbouring farms, tell them the story of the Rebellion, and teach them the tune of *Beasts of England*.

monstrous [mánstrəs / mɔ́n-] adj. 부조리한, 비정상의, 터무니없는
injustice [indʒʌ́stis] n. 부정, 불의
turn out of: 내보내다, 내쫓다
good-for-nothing [gúd-fərnʌ̀θiŋ] adj. 쓸모 없는, 변변치 못한

Most of this time Mr. Jones had spent sitting in the taproom of the Red Lion at Willingdon, complaining to anyone who would listen of the **monstrous injustice** he had suffered in being **turned out of** his property by a pack of **good-for-nothing** animals. The other farmers sympathised in principle, but they did not at

adjoin [ədʒóin] v.
인접하다, 옆에 자리하다
term [tə:rm] n.
사이, 관계
disgraceful [disgréisfəl] adj.
면목 없는, 수치스러운, 불명예스러운
shrewd [ʃru:d] adj.
날카로운, 영리한
drive a hard bargain:
인정사정없는 흥정을 하다

rebellion [ribéljən] n.
모반, 반란, 폭동
scorn [skɔ:rn] v.
경멸하다, 가볍게 여기다
fortnight [fɔ́:rtnàit] n.
2주간
put about:
알리다, 퍼뜨리다

first give him much help. At heart, each of them was secretly wondering whether he could not somehow turn Jones's misfortune to his own advantage. It was lucky that the owners of the two farms which **adjoined** Animal Farm were on permanently bad **terms**. One of them, which was named Foxwood, was a large, neglected, old-fashioned farm, much overgrown by woodland, with all its pastures worn out and its hedges in a **disgraceful** condition. Its owner, Mr. Pilkington, was an easy-going gentleman farmer who spent most of his time in fishing or hunting according to the season. The other farm, which was called Pinchfield, was smaller and better kept. Its owner was a Mr. Frederick, a tough, **shrewd** man, perpetually involved in lawsuits and with a name for **driving hard bargains**. These two disliked each other so much that it was difficult for them to come to any agreement, even in defence of their own interests.

Nevertheless, they were both thoroughly frightened by the **rebellion** on Animal Farm, and very anxious to prevent their own animals from learning too much about it. At first they pretended to laugh to **scorn** the idea of animals managing a farm for themselves. The whole thing would be over in a **fortnight**, they said. They **put** it **about** that the animals on the Manor

Farm (they insisted on calling it the Manor Farm; they would not **tolerate** the name "Animal Farm") were **perpetually** fighting among themselves and were also rapidly starving to death. When time passed and the animals had evidently not starved to death, Frederick and Pilkington **changed their tune** and began to talk of the terrible **wickedness** that now **flourished** on Animal Farm. It was **given out** that the animals there practised cannibalism, tortured one another with redhot horseshoes, and had their females in common. This was what came of rebelling against the laws of Nature, Frederick and Pilkington said.

However, these stories were never fully believed. Rumours of a wonderful farm, where the human beings had been turned out and the animals managed their own affairs, continued to circulate in vague and distorted forms, and throughout that year a wave of rebelliousness ran through the countryside. Bulls which had always been **tractable** suddenly turned savage, sheep broke down hedges and devoured the clover, cows kicked the **pail** over, **hunters** refused their fences and shot their riders on to the other side. Above all, the tune and even the words of *Beasts of England* were known everywhere. It had spread with astonishing speed. The human beings could not contain their rage when they heard this song, though they pretended to think it merely ridiculous. They could not understand, they said, how even animals could bring themselves to sing such **contemptible** rubbish. Any animal caught singing it was given a **flogging on the spot**. And yet the song was **irrepressible**. The blackbirds whistled it in the hedges, the pigeons **cooed** it in the elms, it got into the din of the **smithies** and the tune of the church bells. And when the human beings listened to it, they secretly **trembled**, hearing in it a **prophecy** of their future **doom**.

Early in October, when the corn was cut and stacked and some of it was already **threshed**, a flight of pigeons came whirling through the air and alighted in the yard of Animal Farm in the wildest excitement. Jones and all his men, with half a dozen others from Foxwood and Pinchfield, had entered the five barred gate and were coming up the cart-track that led to the farm. They were all carrying sticks, except Jones, who was marching ahead with a gun in his hands. Obviously they were going to attempt the **recapture** of the farm.

This had long been expected, and all preparations had been made. Snowball, who had studied an old book of Julius Caesar's campaigns which he had found in the farmhouse, was in

---

contemptible [kəntémptəbəl] adj. 멸시할 만한, 경멸할 만한, 비열한
flogging [flágiŋ / flɔ́g-] n. 매질, 태형
on the spot: 그 자리에서, 즉석에서
irrepressible [iriprésəbəl] adj. 억누를 수 없는, 억제할 수 없는
coo [ku:] v. (비둘기 따위가) 꾸꾸꾸 울다
smithy [smíθi, smíði] n. 대장장이의 일터
tremble [trémb-əl] v. 떨다, 떨리다
prophecy [práfəsi / prɔ́-] n. 예언
doom [du:m] n. 운명, 비운, 파멸
thresh [θreʃ] v. 도리깨질하다, 타작하다
recapture [ri:kǽptʃə:r] n. 탈환, 회복

charge of the defensive operations. He gave his orders quickly, and in a couple of minutes every animal was at his post.

As the human beings approached the farm buildings, Snowball launched his first attack. All the pigeons, to the number of thirty-five, flew to and fro over the men's heads and muted upon them from mid air; and while the men were dealing with this, the geese, who had been hiding behind the hedge, rushed out and **pecked** viciously at the calves of their legs. However, this was only a light skirmishing **manoeuvre**, intended to create a little disorder, and the men easily drove the geese off with their sticks. Snowball now launched his second line of attack. Muriel, Benjamin, and all the sheep, with Snowball at the head of them, rushed forward and **prodded** and **butted** the men from every side, while Benjamin turned round and lashed at them with his small hoofs. But once again the men, with their sticks and their hobnailed boots, were too strong for them; and suddenly, at a **squeal** from Snowball, which was the signal for **retreat**, all the animals turned and fled through the gateway into the yard.

The men gave a shout of **triumph**. They saw, as they imagined, their enemies in flight, and they rushed after them in disorder. This was

---

peck [pek] v.
(부리로) 쪼다, 쪼아먹다
maneuver [mənúːvər] n.
작전 행동, 계략, 책략
prod [prɑd / prɔd] v.
찌르다, 쑤시다
butt [bʌt] v.
(머리·뿔 따위로) 받다, 부딪치다
squeal [skwiːl] n.
다소 긴 비명, 꽥 소리
retreat [ritríːt] n.
철수, 후퇴

triumph [tráiəmf] n.
승리, 승리감, 성공의 기쁨

ambush [ǽmbuʃ] n.
매복, 복병
rear [riə:r] n.
뒤, 배후, 후방
charge [tʃɑ:rdʒ] n.
돌격, 진격
stone [stoun] n.
스톤. 무게 단위로서 14파운드 (6.35kg)에 상당함
terrifying [térəfàiŋ] adj.
무서운, 무서워할 만한
spectacle [spéktək-əl] n.
광경, 미관, 장관
stallion [stǽljən] n.
수말, 종마
stretch [stretʃ] v.
뻗게 하다, 때려눕히다, 큰 대자로 뻗게 하다
panic [pǽnik] n.
공황, 공포, 겁먹음
gore [gɔ:r] v.
(뿔, 엄니 따위로) 찌르다, 들이받다

just what Snowball had intended. As soon as they were well inside the yard, the three horses, the three cows, and the rest of the pigs, who had been lying in **ambush** in the cow shed, suddenly emerged in their **rear**, cutting them off. Snowball now gave the signal for the **charge**. He himself dashed straight for Jones. Jones saw him coming, raised his gun and fired. The pellets scored bloody streaks along Snowball's back, and a sheep dropped dead. Without halting for an instant. Snowball flung his fifteen **stone** against Jones's legs. Jones was hurled into a pile of dung and his gun flew out of his hands. But the most **terrifying spectacle** of all was Boxer, rearing up on his hind legs and striking out with his great iron-shod hoofs like a **stallion**. His very first blow took a stable-lad from Foxwood on the skull and **stretched** him lifeless in the mud. At the sight, several men dropped their sticks and tried to run. **Panic** overtook them, and the next moment all the animals together were chasing them round and round the yard. They were **gored**, kicked, bitten, trampled on. There was not an animal on the farm that did not take vengeance on them after his own fashion. Even the cat suddenly leapt off a roof onto a cowman's shoulders and sank her claws in his neck, at which he yelled horribly. At a moment when the opening was clear,

make a bolt for: 내빼다, 도망치다 ignominious [ìgnəmíniəs] adj. 수치스러운, 불명예스러운 retreat [ritríːt] n. 철수, 후퇴	the men were glad enough to rush out of the yard and **make a bolt for** the main road. And so within five minutes of their invasion they were in **ignominious retreat** by the same way as they had come, with a flock of geese hissing after them and pecking at their calves all the way.
paw [pɔː] v. (동물이) 발로 긁다(치다)	All the men were gone except one. Back in the yard Boxer was **pawing** with his hoof at the stable-lad who lay face down in the mud, trying to turn him over. The boy did not stir.
on purpose: 고의로, 일부러	"He is dead." said Boxer sorrowfully. "I had no intention of doing that. I forgot that I was wearing iron shoes. Who will believe that I did not do this **on purpose**?"
sentimentality [sèntəmentǽləti] n. 감상벽, 감상적인 생각	"No **sentimentality**, comrade!" cried Snowball, from whose wounds the blood was still dripping. "War is war. The only good human being is a dead one." "I have no wish to take life, not even human life," repeated Boxer, and his eyes were full of tears.
Snowball now gave the signal for the charge. He himself dashed straight for Jones.	"Where is Mollie?" exclaimed somebody. Mollie in fact was missing. For a moment there was great alarm; it was feared that the men might have harmed her in some way, or even carried her off with them. In the end, however, she was found hiding in her stall with her head buried among the hay in the

manger [méindʒə:r] n.
여물통, 구유
stun [stʌn] v.
기절시키다, 아찔하게 하다,
정신을 잃게 하다
make off:
달아나다, 급히 떠나다
reassemble [rì:əsémb-əl] v.
다시 모으다, 다시 모이다
recount [rikáunt] v.
자세히 말하다, 이야기하다
exploit [éksplɔit, iksplɔ́it] n.
공훈, 공적, 위업
impromptu [imprámptju: / -prɔ́m-] adj.
즉석의, 즉흥의

unanimously [ju:nǽnəməsli] adv. 같은 의견으로, 만장일치로
decoration [dèkəréiʃən] n.
훈장
confer [kənfə́:r] v.
수여하다, 베풀다
there and then:
즉시, 곧장
posthumously [pástʃuməsli / pɔ́s-] adv.
사후에, 죽은 뒤에

manger. She had taken to flight as soon as the gun went off. And when the others came back from looking for her, it was to find that the stable-lad, who in fact was only **stunned**, had already recovered and **made off**.

The animals had now **reassembled** in the wildest excitement, each **recounting** his own **exploits** in the battle at the top of his voice. An **impromptu** celebration of the victory was held immediately. The flag was run up and *Beasts of England* was sung a number of times, then the sheep who had been killed was given a solemn funeral, a hawthorn bush being planted on her grave. At the graveside Snowball made a little speech, emphasising the need for all animals to be ready to die for Animal Farm if need be.

The animals decided **unanimously** to create a military **decoration**, "Animal Hero, First Class," which was **conferred there and then** on Snowball and Boxer. It consisted of a brass medal (they were really some old horse-brasses which had been found in the harness room), to be worn on Sundays and holidays. There was also "Animal Hero, Second Class," which was conferred **posthumously** on the dead sheep.

There was much discussion as to what the battle should be called. In the end, it was named the Battle of the Cowshed, since that was where

artillery [ɑ:rtílərì] n.
포, 대포
anniversary [æ̀nəvə́:rsəri] n.
기념일

the ambush had been sprung. Mr. Jones's gun had been found lying in the mud, and it was known that there was a supply of cartridges in the farmhouse. It was decided to set the gun up at the foot of the flagstaff, like a piece of **artillery**, and to fire it twice a year—once on October the twelfth, the **anniversary** of the Battle of the Cowshed, and once on Midsummer Day, the anniversary of the Rebellion.

At the graveside Snowball made a little speech, emphasising the need for all animals to be ready to die for Animal Farm if need be.

Chapter V

appetite [ǽpitàit] n.
식욕
pretext [príːtekst] n.
핑계, 구실
stroll [stroul] v.
거닐다, 어슬렁거리다, 산책하다
blithely [blaiðli] adv.
즐겁게, 유쾌하게, 쾌활하게
flirt [fləːrt] v.
펄럭펄럭 부치다, 퍼득거리다

As winter drew on, Mollie became more and more troublesome. She was late for work every morning and excused herself by saying that she had overslept, and she complained of mysterious pains, although her **appetite** was excellent. On every kind of **pretext** she would run away from work and go to the drinking pool, where she would stand foolishly gazing at her own reflection in the water. But there were also rumours of something more serious. One day as Mollie **strolled blithely** into the yard, **flirting** her long tail and chewing at a stalk of hay. Clover took her aside.

"Mollie," she said, "I have something very serious to say to you. This morning I saw you

stroke [strouk] v. 쓰다듬다, 어루만지다	looking over the hedge that divides Animal Farm from Foxwood. One of Mr. Pilkington's men was standing on the other side of the hedge. And—I was a long way away, but I am almost certain I saw this—he was talking to you and you were allowing him to **stroke** your nose. What does that mean, Mollie?"

"He didn't! I wasn't! It isn't true!" cried Mollie, beginning to **prance** about and **paw** the ground.

prance [præns, pra:ns] v.
뒷발로 뛰어오르다
paw [pɔ:] v.
(말이) 앞발로 차다

"Mollie! Look me in the face. Do you give me your word of honour that that man was not stroking your nose?"

"It isn't true!" repeated Mollie, but she could not look Clover in the face, and the next moment she **took to her heels** and galloped away into the field.

take to (one's) heels:
도망치다

A thought struck Clover. Without saying anything to the others, she went to Mollie's stall and turned over the straw with her hoof. Hidden under the straw was a little pile of lump sugar and several bunches of ribbon of different colours.

whereabout [hwé-ərəbàuts] n.
소재, 위치, 거처
shaft [ʃæft, ʃɑ:ft] n.
(수레의) 채, 끌채
dogcart [dɔ́(:)gkɑ̀:rt, dág-] n.
경2륜 마차

Three days later Mollie disappeared. For some weeks nothing was known of her **whereabouts**, then the pigeons reported that they had seen her on the other side of Willingdon. She was between the **shafts** of a smart **dogcart** painted red and black, which was standing

breeches [brítʃiz] n.
반바지, 바지
gaiter [géitər] n.
각반(脚絆)
publican [pʌ́blikən] n.
선술집의 주인

ratify [rǽtəfài] v.
비준하다, 재가하다
arrangement [əréindʒmənt] n.
준비, 계획, 조정, 협정
dispute [dispjú:t] n.
토론, 논박, 논쟁
disagreement [dìsəgrí:mənt] n.
불일치, 논쟁, 불화
acreage [éikəridʒ] n.
평수, 면적
following [fálouiŋ / fɔ́l-] n.
추종자, 신봉자, 지지자

outside a public-house. A fat red-faced man in check **breeches** and **gaiters**, who looked like a **publican**, was stroking her nose and feeding her with sugar. Her coat was newly clipped and she wore a scarlet ribbon round her forelock. She appeared to be enjoying herself, so the pigeons said. None of the animals ever mentioned Mollie again.

In January there came bitterly hard weather. The earth was like iron, and nothing could be done in the fields. Many meetings were held in the big barn, and the pigs occupied themselves with planning out the work of the coming season. It had come to be accepted that the pigs, who were manifestly cleverer than the other animals, should decide all questions of farm policy, though their decisions had to be **ratified** by a majority vote. This **arrangement** would have worked well enough if it had not been for the **disputes** between Snowball and Napoleon. These two disagreed at every point where **disagreement** was possible. If one of them suggested sowing a bigger **acreage** with barley, the other was certain to demand a bigger acreage of oats, and if one of them said that such and such a field was just right for cabbages, the other would declare that it was useless for anything except roots. Each had his own **following**, and there were some violent debates. At the Meetings Snowball often won over the majority by his brilliant speeches, but Napoleon was better at **canvassing** support for himself **in between times**. He was especially successful with the sheep. Of late the sheep had taken to bleating "Four legs good, two legs bad" both in and out of season, and they often interrupted the Meeting with this. It was noticed that they were especially liable to break into "Four legs good, two legs bad" at crucial moments in Snowball's speeches. Snowball had made a close study of some **back numbers** of the *Farmer and Stock breeder* which he had found in the farmhouse, and was full of plans for innovations and improvements. He talked **learnedly** about field-drains, **silage**, and basic slag, and had worked out a complicated scheme for all the animals to drop their dung directly in the fields, at a different spot every day, to save the labour of **cartage**. Napoleon produced no schemes of his own, but said quietly that Snowball's would **come to nothing**, and seemed to be **biding his time**. But of all their controversies, none was so bitter as the one that **took place** over the windmill.

In the long pasture, not far from the farm buildings, there was a small knoll which was the highest point on the farm. After surveying the ground. Snowball declared that this was

---

canvass [kǽnvəs] v.
얻으려 하다, 부탁하다
in between times:
(일과 일의) 사이에
back number:
과월호, 지난 잡지
learnedly [lə́:rnidli] adv.
학문적으로, 박식하게
silage [sáilidʒ] n.
사일로(silo)에 저장한 꼴, 저장 목초
cartage [ká:rtidʒ] n.
짐차 수송; 짐차 운송료
come to nothing:
헛수고가 되다, 아무 소용도 없다
bide one's time:
때를 기다리다
take place:
발생하다, 일어나다

Napoleon produced no schemes of his own, but said quietly that Snowball's would come to nothing, and seemed to be biding his time.

dynamo [dáinəmòu] n.
발전기
chaffcutter [tʃǽfkʌtər / tʃɑ́:f-] n. 작두
primitive [prímətiv] adj.
원시적인, 소박한, 유치한
conjure up:
(상상으로) 만들어내다, 상기시키다, 출현시키다
graze [greiz] v.
(가축 등이 풀을) 뜯어먹다,

study [stʌ́di] n.
서재, 연구실
incubator [íŋkjəbèitər, íŋ-] n.
부화기, 부란기
closet [klázit / klɔ́z-] v.
들어앉다, 틀어박히다

just the place for a windmill, which could be made to operate a **dynamo** and supply the farm with electrical power. This would light the stalls and warm them in winter, and would also run a circular saw, a **chaff-cutter**, a mangel-slicer, and an electric milking machine. The animals had never heard of anything of this kind before (for the farm was an old-fashioned one and had only the most **primitive** machinery), and they listened in astonishment while Snowball **conjured up** pictures of fantastic machines which would do their work for them while they **grazed** at their ease in the fields or improved their minds with reading and conversation.

Within a few weeks Snowball's plans for the windmill were fully worked out. The mechanical details came mostly from three books which had belonged to Mr. Jones—*One Thousand Useful Things to Do About the House*, *Every Man His Own Bricklayer*, and *Electricity for Beginners*. Snowball used as his **study** a shed which had once been used for **incubators** and had a smooth wooden floor, suitable for drawing on. He was **closeted** there for hours at a time. With his books held open by a stone, and with a piece of chalk gripped between the knuckles of his trotter, he would move rapidly to and fro, drawing in line after line and uttering

whimper [hwímpə:r] n.
흐느낌, 훌쩍이는 소리
crank [kræŋk] n.
크랭크 (왕복 운동을 회전 운동으로 바꾸거나 그 반대의 일을 하는 기계 장치)
cogwheel [kághwì:l / kɔ́g-] n.
톱니바퀴
unintelligible [ʌ̀nintélədʒəbəl] adj. 알기 힘든, 난해한
be at pains:
~을 하려 노력하다, ~하고자 애쓰다
hold aloof:
관여하지 않다, 관심을 두지 않다
contemplate [kántəmplèit / kɔ́ntem-] v.
눈여겨 보다, 주의 깊게 관찰하다

quarry [kwɔ́:ri / kwári] v.
떠내다, 파내다
sail [seil] n.
돛 모양의 것; 풍차의 날개
procure [proukjúər, prə-] v.
입수하다, 손에 넣다, 획득하다

little **whimpers** of excitement. Gradually the plans grew into a complicated mass of **cranks** and **cog-wheels**, covering more than half the floor, which the other animals found completely **unintelligible** but very impressive. All of them came to look at Snowball's drawings at least once a day. Even the hens and ducks came, and **were at pains** not to tread on the chalk marks. Only Napoleon **held aloof**. He had declared himself against the windmill from the start. One day, however, he arrived unexpectedly to examine the plans. He walked heavily round the shed, looked closely at every detail of the plans and snuffed at them once or twice, then stood for a little while **contemplating** them out of the corner of his eye; then suddenly he lifted his leg, urinated over the plans, and walked out without uttering a word.

The whole farm was deeply divided on the subject of the windmill. Snowball did not deny that to build it would be a difficult business. Stone would have to be **quarried** and built up into walls, then the **sails** would have to be made and after that there would be need for dynamos and cables. (How these were to be **procured**. Snowball did not say.) But he maintained that it could all be done in a year. And thereafter, he declared, so much labour would be saved that the animals would only need to

faction [fǽkʃən] n.
도당, 당파, 파벌
slogan [slóugən] n.
(정당, 단체 따위의) 슬로건, 표어
manger [méindʒəːr] n.
여물통, 구유
side [said] v.
찬성하다, 지지하다, 편들다

determined [ditə́ːrmind] adj.
결심한, 결의가 굳은, 단호한
recapture [riːkǽptʃəːr] v.
되찾다, 탈환하다
reinstate [rìːinstéit] v.
본래대로 하다, 복위시키다
restive [réstiv] adj.
다루기 힘든, 고집센

work three days a week. Napoleon, on the other hand, argued that the great need of the moment was to increase food production, and that if they wasted time on the windmill they would all starve to death. The animals formed themselves into two **factions** under the **slogans**, "Vote for Snowball and the three-day week" and "Vote for Napoleon and the full **manger**." Benjamin was the only animal who did not **side** with either faction. He refused to believe either that food would become more plentiful or that the windmill would save work. Windmill or no windmill, he said, life would go on as it had always gone on—that is, badly.

Apart from the disputes over the windmill, there was the question of the defence of the farm. It was fully realised that though the human beings had been defeated in the Battle of the Cowshed they might make another and more **determined** attempt to **recapture** the farm and **reinstate** Mr. Jones. They had all the more reason for doing so because the news of their defeat had spread across the countryside and made the animals on the neighbouring farms more **restive** than ever. As usual. Snowball and Napoleon were in disagreement. According to Napoleon, what the animals must do was to procure firearms and train themselves in the use of them. According to Snowball, they must send out more and more pigeons and stir up rebellion among the animals on the other farms. The one argued that if they could not defend themselves they **were bound to** be conquered, the other argued that if rebellions happened everywhere they would have no need to defend themselves. The animals listened first to Napoleon, then to Snowball, and could not make up their minds which was right; indeed, they always found themselves in agreement with the one who was speaking at the moment.

At last the day came when Snowball's plans were completed. At the Meeting on the following Sunday the question of whether or not to begin work on the windmill was to be put to the vote. When the animals had assembled in the big barn, Snowball stood up and, though occasionally interrupted by bleating from the sheep, **set forth** his reasons for **advocating** the building of the windmill. Then Napoleon stood up to reply. He said very quietly that the windmill was nonsense and that he advised nobody to vote for it, and promptly sat down again; he had spoken for barely thirty seconds, and seemed almost **indifferent as to** the effect he produced. At this Snowball sprang to his feet, and shouting down the sheep, who had begun bleating again, broke into a passionate

eloquence [éləkwəns] n.
웅변, 능변
carry away:
넋을 잃게 하다, 열광하게 하다
sordid [sɔ́:rdid] adj.
비천한, 불행한, 한심한
harrow [hǽrou] n.
써레
reapers and binders:
(농업) 베어서 단으로 묶는 기계, 바인더
sidelong [-lɔ̀:ŋ / -lɔ̀ŋ] adj.
옆의, 옆으로 향한, 비스듬한
whimper [hwímpə:r] n.
흐느낌, 우는 소리

bound [baund] v.
뛰어가다, 약진하다
dash [dæʃ] v.
격렬하게 움직이다, 돌진하다, 급히 가다
just in time:
겨우 빠듯하게, 가까스로

appeal in favour of the windmill. Until now the animals had been about equally divided in their sympathies, but in a moment Snowball's **eloquence** had **carried** them **away**. In glowing sentences he painted a picture of Animal Farm as it might be when **sordid** labour was lifted from the animals' backs. His imagination had now run far beyond chaff-cutters and turnip-slicers. Electricity, he said, could operate threshing machines, ploughs, **harrows**, rollers, and **reapers and binders**, besides supplying every stall with its own electric light, hot and cold water, and an electric heater. By the time he had finished speaking, there was no doubt as to which way the vote would go. But just at this moment Napoleon stood up and, casting a peculiar **sidelong** look at Snowball, uttered a high-pitched **whimper** of a kind no one had ever heard him utter before.

At this there was a terrible baying sound outside, and nine enormous dogs wearing brass-studded collars came **bounding** into the barn. They **dashed** straight for Snowball, who only sprang from his place **just in time** to escape their snapping jaws. In a moment he was out of the door and they were after him. Too amazed and frightened to speak, all the animals crowded through the door to watch the chase. Snowball was racing across the long pasture that led to the road. He was running as only a pig can run, but the dogs were close **on his heels.** Suddenly he slipped and it seemed certain that they had him. Then he was up again, running faster than ever, then the dogs were gaining on him again. One of them all but closed his jaws on Snowball's tail, but Snowball whisked it free just in time. Then he put on an extra **spurt** and, with a few inches to spare, slipped through a hole in the hedge and was seen no more.

Silent and terrified, the animals crept back into the barn. In a moment the dogs came bounding back. At first no one had been able to imagine where these creatures came from, but the problem was soon solved: they were the puppies whom Napoleon had taken away from their mothers and **reared** privately. Though not yet full-grown, they were huge dogs, and as fierce-looking as wolves. They kept close to Napoleon. It was noticed that they wagged their tails to him in the same way as the other dogs had been used to do to Mr. Jones.

Napoleon, with the dogs following him, now mounted on to the raised portion of the floor where Major had previously stood to deliver his speech. He announced that from now on the Sunday-morning Meetings would **come to an end**. They were unnecessary, he said, and

---

on one's heels:
누구를 뒤쫓아
spurt [spəːrt] n.
분발, 역주

They dashed straight for Snowball, who only sprang from his place just in time to escape their snapping jaws.

rear [riər] v.
기르다, 사육하다, 육성하다

come to an end:
멈추다, 끝내다

preside [prizáid] v.
사회를 하다, 의장을 맡다

Napoleon, with the dogs following him, now mounted on to the raised portion of the floor ...

expulsion [ikspʌ́lʃən] n.
추방, 배제, 제명
dismay [disméi] v.
놀라게 하다, 불안하게 하다, 당황케 하다
marshal [má:rʃ-əl] v.
모으다, 정리하다
articulate [ɑ:rtíkjəlit] adj.
명확한, 분명한
squeal [skwi:l] n.
다소 긴 비명, 꽥 소리
disapproval [dìsəprú:vəl] n.
반대 의견, 불만, 비난
menacing [ménəsiŋ] adj.
위협적인
growl [graul] v.
으르렁거림, 으르렁 소리

wasted time. In future all questions relating to the working of the farm would be settled by a special committee of pigs, **presided** over by himself. These would meet in private and afterwards communicate their decisions to the others. The animals would still assemble on Sunday mornings to salute the flag, sing *Beasts of England*, and receive their orders for the week; but there would be no more debates.

In spite of the shock that Snowball's **expulsion** had given them, the animals were **dismayed** by this announcement. Several of them would have protested if they could have found the right arguments. Even Boxer was vaguely troubled. He set his ears back, shook his forelock several times, and tried hard to **marshal** his thoughts; but in the end he could not think of anything to say. Some of the pigs themselves, however, were more **articulate**. Four young porkers in the front row uttered shrill **squeals** of **disapproval**, and all four of them sprang to their feet and began speaking at once. But suddenly the dogs sitting round Napoleon let out deep, **menacing growls**, and the pigs fell silent and sat down again. Then the sheep broke out into a tremendous bleating of "Four legs good, two legs bad!" which went on for nearly a quarter of an hour and put an end to any chance of discussion.

Afterwards Squealer was sent round the farm to explain the new arrangement to the others.

"Comrades," he said, "I trust that every animal here **appreciates** the sacrifice that Comrade Napoleon has made in taking this extra labour upon himself. Do not imagine, comrades, that leadership is a pleasure! **On the contrary**, it is a deep and heavy responsibility. No one believes more firmly than Comrade Napoleon that all animals are equal. He would be only too happy to let you make your decisions for yourselves. But sometimes you might make the wrong decisions, comrades, and then where should we be? Suppose you had decided to follow Snowball, with his **moonshine** of windmills—Snowball, who, as we now know, was no better than a criminal?"

"He fought bravely at the Battle of the Cowshed," said somebody.

"Bravery is not enough," said Squealer. "Loyalty and obedience are more important. And as to the Battle of the Cowshed, I believe the time will come when we shall find that Snowball's part in it was much **exaggerated**. **Discipline**, comrades, **iron** discipline! That is the **watchword** for today. One false step, and our enemies would be upon us. Surely, comrades, you do not want Jones back?"

---

appreciate [əpríːʃièit] v.
평가하다, 인정하다, 헤아리다
on the contrary:
반대로
moonshine [múːnʃàin] n.
헛소리, 쓸데없는 공상

exaggerate [igzǽdʒərèit] v.
과장하다, 침소봉대하다
discipline [dísəplin] n.
훈련, 규율, 풍기
iron [áiərn] adj.
철의, (철같이) 굳은, 확고한
watchword [wátʃwə̀ːrd] n.
(정당 따위의) 표어, 슬로건

unanswerable [ʌnǽnsərəbə́l] adj. 대답할 수 없는, 반박할 수 없는, 다툴 여지가 없는
liable [láiəb-əl] adj. 자칫하면 ~하는, ~하기 쉬운

"... Discipline, comrades, iron discipline! That is the watchword for today. One false step, and our enemies would be upon us. ..."

rub off: 문질러 없애다, 비벼서 벗기다
disinter [dìsintə́:r] v. 파내다, 발굴하다
reverent [rév-ərənt] adj. 경건한, 공손한

And from then on he adopted the maxim, "Napoleon is always right," in addition to his private motto of "I will work harder."

Once again this argument was **unanswerable**. Certainly the animals did not want Jones back; if the holding of debates on Sunday mornings was **liable** to bring him back, then the debates must stop. Boxer, who had now had time to think things over, voiced the general feeling by saying: "If Comrade Napoleon says it, it must be right." And from then on he adopted the maxim, "Napoleon is always right," in addition to his private motto of "I will work harder."

By this time the weather had broken and the spring ploughing had begun. The shed where Snowball had drawn his plans of the windmill had been shut up and it was assumed that the plans had been **rubbed off** the floor. Every Sunday morning at ten o'clock the animals assembled in the big barn to receive their orders for the week. The skull of old Major, now clean of flesh, had been **disinterred** from the orchard and set up on a stump at the foot of the flagstaff, beside the gun. After the hoisting of the flag, the animals were required to file past the skull in a **reverent** manner before entering the barn. Nowadays they did not sit all together as they had done in the past. Napoleon, with Squealer and another pig named Minimus, who had a remarkable gift for composing songs and poems, sat on the front of the

gruff [grʌf] adj.
거친, 걸걸한
disperse [dispə́:rs] v.
흩어지다, 헤어지다

expulsion [ikspʌ́lʃən] n.
추방, 배제, 제명
ration [ræʃ-ən, réi-] n.
(식품 등의) 배급, 식량

advocate [ǽdvəkèit] v.
주장하다, 변호하다

raised platform, with the nine young dogs forming a semicircle round them, and the other pigs sitting behind. The rest of the animals sat facing them in the main body of the barn. Napoleon read out the orders for the week in a **gruff** soldierly style, and after a single singing of *Beasts of England*, all the animals **dispersed**.

On the third Sunday after Snowball's **expulsion**, the animals were somewhat surprised to hear Napoleon announce that the windmill was to be built after all. He did not give any reason for having changed his mind, but merely warned the animals that this extra task would mean very hard work; it might even be necessary to reduce their **rations**. The plans, however, had all been prepared, down to the last detail. A special committee of pigs had been at work upon them for the past three weeks. The building of the windmill, with various other improvements, was expected to take two years.

That evening Squealer explained privately to the other animals that Napoleon had never in reality been opposed to the windmill. On the contrary, it was he who had **advocated** it in the beginning, and the plan which Snowball had drawn on the floor of the incubator shed had actually been stolen from among Napoleon's papers. The windmill was, in fact, Napoleon's own creation. Why, then, asked somebody, had

sly [slai] adj.
교활한, 음흉한, 비열한
maneuver [mənúːvəːr] n.
작전 행동, 계략, 책략
out of the way:
비켜선, 방해가 되지 않는
interference [ìntərfíərəns] n.
방해, 훼방, 간섭
tactics [tæktiks] n.
작전, 수단, 책략
persuasively [pərswéisivli]
adv. 설득력 있게, 구변이 좋게
growl [graul] v.
으르렁거리다

he spoken so strongly against it? Here Squealer looked very **sly**. That, he said, was Comrade Napoleon's cunning. He had *seemed* to oppose the windmill, simply as a **manoeuvre** to get rid of Snowball, who was a dangerous character and a bad influence. Now that Snowball was **out of the way**, the plan could go forward without his **interference**. This, said Squealer, was something called **tactics**. He repeated a number of times, "Tactics, comrades, tactics!" skipping round and whisking his tail with a merry laugh. The animals were not certain what the word meant, but Squealer spoke so **persuasively**, and the three dogs who happened to be with him **growled** so threateningly, that they accepted his explanation without further questions.

He repeated a number of times, "Tactics, comrades, tactics!" skipping round and whisking his tail with a merry laugh.

Chapter VI

grudge [grʌdʒ] v.
꺼리다, 아까워하다

voluntary [váləntèri / vɔ́ləntəri] adj.
자발적인, 지원의
absent [æbsént] v.
자리를 비우다, 결석하다

All that year the animals worked like slaves. But they were happy in their work; they **grudged** no effort or sacrifice, well aware that everything that they did was for the benefit of themselves and those of their kind who would come after them, and not for a pack of idle, thieving human beings.

Throughout the spring and summer they worked a sixty-hour week, and in August Napoleon announced that there would be work on Sunday afternoons as well. This work was strictly **voluntary**, but any animal who **absented** himself from it would have his rations reduced by half. Even so, it was found necessary to leave certain tasks undone. The harvest was

foresee [fɔːrsíː] v.
예견하다, 앞일을 내다보다

quarry [kwɔ́ːri / kwɑ́ri] n.
채석장
outhouse [áuthàus] n.
딴채, 헛간
at hand:
손이 닿는 곳에, 가까이에; 언제든지 쓸 수 있게
pick [pik] n.
곡괭이
crowbar [˗bɑ̀ːr] n.
쇠지레
utilize, utilise [júːtəlàiz] v.
이용하다, 활용하다
boulder [bóuldəːr] n.
둥근 돌, 바위
topple [tɑ́p-əl / tɔ́p-əl] v.
쓰러뜨리다, 흔들리게 하다, 전복시키다

a little less successful than in the previous year, and two fields which should have been sown with roots in the early summer were not sown because the ploughing had not been completed early enough. It was possible to **foresee** that the coming winter would be a hard one.

The windmill presented unexpected difficulties. There was a good **quarry** of limestone on the farm, and plenty of sand and cement had been found in one of the **outhouses**, so that all the materials for building were **at hand**. But the problem the animals could not at first solve was how to break up the stone into pieces of suitable size. There seemed no way of doing this except with **picks** and **crowbars**, which no animal could use, because no animal could stand on his hind legs. Only after weeks of vain effort did the right idea occur to somebody—namely, to **utilise** the force of gravity. Huge **boulders**, far too big to be used as they were, were lying all over the bed of the quarry. The animals lashed ropes round these, and then all together, cows, horses, sheep, any animal that could lay hold of the rope—even the pigs sometimes joined in at critical moments—they dragged them with desperate slowness up the slope to the top of the quarry, where they were **toppled** over the edge, to shatter to pieces below. Transporting the stone when it was once

yoke [jouk] v.
멍에를 얹다
superintendence
[sù:pərinténdəns] n.
감독, 지휘

laborious [ləbɔ́:riəs] adj.
힘드는, 고된, 애쓴
strain [strein] v.
무리하게 사용하다, 전력을 다하다
overstrain [òuvərstréin] v.
너무 쓰다, 무리하다

broken was comparatively simple. The horses carried it off in cart-loads, the sheep dragged single blocks, even Muriel and Benjamin **yoked** themselves into an old governess-cart and did their share. By late summer a sufficient store of stone had accumulated, and then the building began, under the **superintendence** of the pigs.

But it was a slow, **laborious** process. Frequently it took a whole day of exhausting effort to drag a single boulder to the top of the quarry, and sometimes when it was pushed over the edge it failed to break. Nothing could have been achieved without Boxer, whose strength seemed equal to that of all the rest of the animals put together. When the boulder began to slip and the animals cried out in despair at finding themselves dragged down the hill, it was always Boxer who **strained** himself against the rope and brought the boulder to a stop. To see him toiling up the slope inch by inch, his breath coming fast, the tips of his hoofs clawing at the ground, and his great sides matted with sweat, filled everyone with admiration. Clover warned him sometimes to be careful not to **overstrain** himself, but Boxer would never listen to her. His two slogans, "I will work harder" and "Napoleon is always right," seemed to him a sufficient answer to all problems. He had made arrangements with the cockerel to call him three-quarters of an hour earlier in the mornings instead of half an hour. And in his spare moments, of which there were not many nowadays, he would go alone to the quarry, collect a load of broken stone, and drag it down to the site of the windmill unassisted.

The animals were not **badly off** throughout that summer, **in spite of** the hardness of their work. If they had no more food than they had had in Jones's day, at least they did not have less. The advantage of only having to feed themselves, and not having to support five **extravagant** human beings as well, was so great that it would have taken a lot of failures to **outweigh** it. And in many ways the animal method of doing things was more efficient and saved labour. Such jobs as weeding, for instance, could be done with a thoroughness impossible to human beings. And again, since no animal now stole, it was unnecessary to fence off pasture from **arable** land, which saved a lot of labour on the **upkeep** of hedges and gates. Nevertheless, as the summer wore on, various **unforeseen shortages** began to make themselves felt. There was need of paraffin oil, nails, string, dog biscuits, and iron for the horses' shoes, none of which could be produced on the farm. Later there would also be need for seeds

---

badly off:
불리한, 가난한, 곤궁한
in spite of:
~에도 불구하고
extravagant [ikstrǽvəgənt] adj. 터무니없는, 지나친, 엉뚱한
outweigh [àutwéi] v.
보다 뛰어나다, 보다 중요하다
arable [ǽrəbəl] adj.
경작에 알맞은, 개간할 수 있는
upkeep [ʌ́pkìːp] n.
유지; 유지비
unforeseen [ʌnfɔːrsíːn] adj.
예기치 않은, 의외의
shortage [ʃɔ́ːrtidʒ] n.
부족, 결핍

and artificial manures, besides various tools and, finally, the machinery for the windmill. How these were to be procured, no one was able to imagine.

One Sunday morning, when the animals assembled to receive their orders, Napoleon announced that he had decided upon a new policy. From now onwards Animal Farm would engage in trade with the neighbouring farms: not, of course, for any commercial purpose, but simply in order to obtain certain materials which were urgently necessary. The needs of the windmill must **override** everything else, he said. He was therefore making **arrangements** to sell a stack of hay and part of the current year's wheat crop, and later on, if more money were needed, it would have to be made up by the sale of eggs, for which there was always a market in Willingdon. The hens, said Napoleon, should welcome this sacrifice as their own special **contribution** towards the building of the windmill.

Once again the animals were conscious of a vague **uneasiness**. Never to have any dealings with human beings, never to engage in trade, never to make use of money—had not these been among the earliest **resolutions** passed at that first triumphant Meeting after Jones was expelled? All the animals remembered passing

abolish [əbáliʃ / əbɔ́l-] v.
폐지하다, 철폐하다, 완전히 파괴하다
timidly [tímidli] adv.
두려워하며, 소심하게
solicitor [səlísətə:r] n.
변호사
intermediary [intərmí:dièri] n.
중개자

at rest:
안심하여, 마음 놓이게
traceable [tréisəb-əl] adj.
찾아낼 수 있는, ~에 기인하는

such resolutions: or at least they thought that they remembered it. The four young pigs who had protested when Napoleon **abolished** the Meetings raised their voices **timidly**, but they were promptly silenced by a tremendous growling from the dogs. Then, as usual, the sheep broke into "Four legs good, two legs bad!" and the momentary awkwardness was smoothed over. Finally Napoleon raised his trotter for silence and announced that he had already made all the arrangements. There would be no need for any of the animals to come in contact with human beings, which would clearly be most undesirable. He intended to take the whole burden upon his own shoulders. A Mr. Whymper, a **solicitor** living in Willingdon, had agreed to act as **intermediary** between Animal Farm and the outside world, and would visit the farm every Monday morning to receive his instructions. Napoleon ended his speech with his usual cry of "Long live Animal Farm!", and after the singing of *Beasts of England* the animals were dismissed.

Afterwards Squealer made a round of the farm and set the animals' minds **at rest**. He assured them that the resolution against engaging in trade and using money had never been passed, or even suggested. It was pure imagination, probably **traceable** in the

shrewdly [ʃru:dli] adv.
빈틈없이, 기민하게

broker [bróukər] n.
중개인, 브로커
commission [kəmíʃən] n.
위임, 위탁, 대리 업무; 수수료
dread [dred] n.
불안, 공포
article of faith:
굳은 신념, 신조
go bankrupt:
파산하다
sooner or later:
머지않아, 언젠가는, 결국에는

beginning to lies circulated by Snowball. A few animals still felt faintly doubtful, but Squealer asked them **shrewdly**, "Are you certain that this is not something that you have dreamed, comrades? Have you any record of such a resolution? Is it written down anywhere?" And since it was certainly true that nothing of the kind existed in writing, the animals were satisfied that they had been mistaken.

Every Monday Mr. Whymper visited the farm as had been arranged. He was a sly-looking little man with side whiskers, a solicitor in a very small way of business, but sharp enough to have realised earlier than anyone else that Animal Farm would need a **broker** and that the **commissions** would be worth having. The animals watched his coming and going with a kind of **dread**, and avoided him as much as possible. Nevertheless, the sight of Napoleon, on all fours, delivering orders to Whymper, who stood on two legs, roused their pride and partly reconciled them to the new arrangement. Their relations with the human race were now not quite the same as they had been before. The human beings did not hate Animal Farm any less now that it was prospering; indeed, they hated it more than ever. Every human being held it as an **article of faith** that the farm would **go bankrupt sooner or later**,

efficiency [ifíʃənsi] n.
능률, 능력, 유능
symptom [símptəm] n.
징후, 조짐, 전조

convince [kənvíns] v.
납득시키다, 확신시키다

and, above all, that the windmill would be a failure. They would meet in the public-houses and prove to one another by means of diagrams that the windmill was bound to fall down, or that if it did stand up, then that it would never work. And yet, against their will, they had developed a certain respect for the **efficiency** with which the animals were managing their own affairs. One **symptom** of this was that they had begun to call Animal Farm by its proper name and ceased to pretend that it was called the Manor Farm. They had also dropped their championship of Jones, who had given up hope of getting his farm back and gone to live in another part of the county. Except through Whymper, there was as yet no contact between Animal Farm and the outside world, but there were constant rumours that Napoleon was about to enter into a definite business agreement either with Mr. Pilkington of Foxwood or with Mr. Frederick of Pinchfield— but never, it was noticed, with both simultaneously.

It was about this time that the pigs suddenly moved into the farmhouse and took up their residence there. Again the animals seemed to remember that a resolution against this had been passed in the early days, and again Squealer was able to **convince** them that this was not the case. It was absolutely necessary,

dignity [dígnəti] n.
위엄, 존엄성, 품위, 긍지
take to:
습관이 되다
sty [stai] n.
돼지우리
ruling [rú:liŋ] n.
공식적인 결정, 재정, 판정, 판결

he said, that the pigs, who were the brains of the farm, should have a quiet place to work in. It was also more suited to the **dignity** of the Leader (for of late he had **taken to** speaking of Napoleon under the title of "Leader") to live in a house than in a mere **sty**. Nevertheless, some of the animals were disturbed when they heard that the pigs not only took their meals in the kitchen and used the drawing-room as a recreation room, but also slept in the beds. Boxer passed it off as usual with "Napoleon is always right!", but Clover, who thought she remembered a definite **ruling** against beds, went to the end of the barn and tried to puzzle out the Seven Commandments which were inscribed there. Finding herself unable to read more than individual letters, she fetched Muriel.

"Muriel," she said, "read me the Fourth Commandment. Does it not say something about never sleeping in a bed?"

With some difficulty Muriel spelt it out.

"It says, 'No animal shall sleep in a bed *with sheets*'" she announced finally.

"It says, 'No animal shall sleep in a bed *with sheets*'" she announced finally.

Curiously enough, Clover had not remembered that the Fourth Commandment mentioned sheets; but as it was there on the wall, it must have done so. And Squealer, who happened to be passing at this moment, attended by two or three dogs, was able to put the whole matter

perspective [pə:rspéktiv] n.
전망, 시각, 견지
brainwork [bréinwə̀:rk] n.
머리 쓰는 일, 정신 노동
repose [ripóuz] n.
휴식, 고요함, 침착

reassure [rì:əʃúə:r] v.
안심시키다, 기운을 돋우다

none too:
조금도 ~하지 않다, 결코 ~하지 않다

in its proper **perspective**.

"You have heard, then, comrades," he said, "that we pigs now sleep in the beds of the farmhouse? And why not? You did not suppose, surely, that there was ever a ruling against *beds*? A bed merely means a place to sleep in. A pile of straw in a stall is a bed, properly regarded. The rule was against *sheets*, which are a human invention. We have removed the sheets from the farmhouse beds, and sleep between blankets. And very comfortable beds they are too! But not more comfortable than we need, I can tell you, comrades, with all the **brainwork** we have to do nowadays. You would not rob us of our **repose**, would you, comrades? You would not have us too tired to carry out our duties? Surely none of you wishes to see Jones back?"

The animals **reassured** him on this point immediately, and no more was said about the pigs sleeping in the farmhouse beds. And when, some days afterwards, it was announced that from now on the pigs would get up an hour later in the mornings than the other animals, no complaint was made about that either.

By the autumn the animals were tired but happy. They had had a hard year, and after the sale of part of the hay and corn, the stores of food for the winter were **none too** plentiful, but the windmill **compensated** for everything. It was almost half built now. After the harvest there was a **stretch** of clear dry weather, and the animals toiled harder than ever, thinking it well worth while to **plod to and fro** all day with blocks of stone if by doing so they could raise the walls another foot. Boxer would even come out at nights and work for an hour or two on his own by the light of the **harvest moon**. In their spare moments the animals would walk round and round the half-finished mill, admiring the strength and perpendicularity of its walls and **marvelling** that they should ever have been able to build anything so **imposing**. Only old Benjamin refused to grow enthusiastic about the windmill, though, as usual, he would utter nothing beyond the **cryptic** remark that donkeys live a long time.

November came, with raging south-west winds. Building had to stop because it was now too wet to mix the cement. Finally there came a night when the **gale** was so violent that the farm buildings rocked on their foundations and several tiles were blown off the roof of the barn. The hens woke up **squawking** with terror because they had all dreamed simultaneously of hearing a gun go off in the distance. In the morning the animals came out of their stalls to find that the **flagstaff** had been blown

---

compensate [kámpənsèit / kóm-] v.
보상하다, 벌충하다, 상쇄하다
stretch [stretʃ] n.
(연속된) 길, 거리, 넓이, 범위, 일련의 기간
plod [plɑd / plɔd] v.
열심히 일하다
to and fro:
앞뒤로, 이리저리
harvest moon:
중추의 만월
marvel [má:rv-əl] v.
놀라다, 경탄하다
imposing [impóuziŋ] adj.
위압하는, 당당한, 훌륭한
cryptic [kríptik] adj.
숨은, 비밀의, 수수께끼 같은

gale [geil] n.
센바람, 강풍
squawk [skwɔ:k] v.
(새 따위가) 꽥꽥 울다
flagstaff [flǽgstæf, flǽgstɑ:f] n. 깃대, 국기 게양대

down and an elm tree at the foot of the orchard had been plucked up like a radish. They had just noticed this when a cry of despair broke from every animal's throat. A terrible sight had met their eyes. The windmill was in ruins.

With one accord they dashed down to the spot. Napoleon, who seldom moved out of a walk, raced ahead of them all. Yes, there it lay, the **fruit** of all their struggles, **levelled** to its foundations, the stones they had broken and carried so laboriously scattered all around. Unable at first to speak, they stood gazing **mournfully** at the **litter** of fallen stone. Napoleon paced to and fro in silence, occasionally snuffing at the ground. His tail had grown rigid and twitched sharply from side to side, a sign in him of intense mental activity. Suddenly he halted as though his mind were made up.

"Comrades,' he said quietly, "do you know who is responsible for this? Do you know the enemy who has come in the night and overthrown our windmill? SNOWBALL!" he suddenly roared in a voice of thunder. "Snowball has done this thing! In sheer **malignity**, thinking to **set back** our plans and **avenge** himself for his **ignominious expulsion**, this **traitor** has crept here under cover of night and destroyed our work of nearly a year. Comrades, here and

pronounce [prənáuns] v.
언도하다, 선고하다
bring to justice:
재판에 회부하다, 처벌하다

beyond measure:
엄청나게
indignation [ìndignéiʃən] n.
분개, 분노

rain or shine:
비가 오거나 말거나, 어떤 일이 있어도
undo [ʌndú:] v.
망치다, 파멸시키다, 몰락하게 하다
alteration [ɔ̀:ltəréiʃən] n.
변경, 개조

now I **pronounce** the death sentence upon Snowball. 'Animal Hero, Second Class,' and half a bushel of apples to any animal who **brings him to justice**. A full bushel to anyone who captures him alive!"

The animals were shocked **beyond measure** to learn that even Snowball could be guilty of such an action. There was a cry of **indignation**, and everyone began thinking out ways of catching Snowball if he should ever come back. Almost immediately the footprints of a pig were discovered in the grass at a little distance from the knoll. They could only be traced for a few yards, but appeared to lead to a hole in the hedge. Napoleon snuffed deeply at them and pronounced them to be Snowball's. He gave it as his opinion that Snowball had probably come from the direction of Foxwood Farm.

"No more delays, comrades!" cried Napoleon when the footprints had been examined. "There is work to be done. This very morning we begin rebuilding the windmill, and we will build all through the winter, **rain or shine**. We will teach this miserable traitor that he cannot **undo** our work so easily. Remember, comrades, there must be no **alteration** in our plans: they shall be carried out to the day. Forward, comrades! Long live the windmill! Long live Animal Farm!"

Chapter VII

sleet [sli:t] n.
진눈깨비
envious [énviəs] adj.
부러워하는, 질투심이 강한
rejoice [ridʒóis] v.
기뻐하다
triumph [tráiəmf] v.
승리를 거두다, 이기다, 의기
양양해 하다
on time:
정각에, 제시간에

spite [spait] n.
악의, 심술, 앙심

It was a bitter winter. The stormy weather was followed by **sleet** and snow, and then by a hard frost which did not break till well into February. The animals carried on as best they could with the rebuilding of the windmill, well knowing that the outside world was watching them and that the **envious** human beings would **rejoice** and **triumph** if the mill were not finished **on time**.

Out of **spite**, the human beings pretended not to believe that it was Snowball who had destroyed the windmill: they said that it had fallen down because the walls were too thin. The animals knew that this was not the case. Still, it had been decided to build the walls three feet thick this time instead of eighteen inches as before, which meant collecting much larger quantities of stone. For a long time the quarry was full of **snowdrifts** and nothing could be done. Some progress was made in the dry frosty weather that followed, but it was cruel work, and the animals could not feel so hopeful about it as they had felt before. They were always cold, and usually hungry as well. Only Boxer and Clover never **lost heart**. Squealer made excellent speeches on the joy of service and the dignity of labour, but the other animals found more **inspiration** in Boxer's strength and his never-failing cry of "I will work harder!"

In January food fell short. The corn ration was **drastically** reduced, and it was announced that an extra potato ration would be issued to **make up for** it. Then it was discovered that the greater part of the potato crop had been frosted in the **clamps**, which had not been covered thickly enough. The potatoes had become soft and discoloured, and only a few were **edible**. For days at a time the animals had nothing to eat but chaff and **mangels**. Starvation seemed to **stare** them **in the face**.

It was vitally necessary to conceal this fact from the outside world. **Emboldened** by the collapse of the windmill, the human beings

put about:
(소문이나 정보 등을) 퍼뜨리다, 알리다
famine [fǽmin] n.
기근, 굶주림, 기아
hitherto [hìðərtú:] adv.
지금까지
pretext [prí:tekst] n.
핑계, 구실
glimpse [glimps] n.
언뜻 눈에 띄임, 흘끗 보기

procure [proukjúər, prə-] v.
입수하다, 손에 넣다, 획득하다
rarely [réə:rli] adv.
드물게, 좀처럼 ~하지 않는

were inventing fresh lies about Animal Farm. Once again it was being **put about** that all the animals were dying of **famine** and disease, and that they were continually fighting among themselves and had resorted to cannibalism and infanticide. Napoleon was well aware of the bad results that might follow if the real facts of the food situation were known, and he decided to make use of Mr. Whymper to spread a contrary impression. **Hitherto** the animals had had little or no contact with Whymper on his weekly visits: now, however, a few selected animals, mostly sheep, were instructed to remark casually in his hearing that rations had been increased. In addition, Napoleon ordered the almost empty bins in the store-shed to be filled nearly to the brim with sand, which was then covered up with what remained of the grain and meal. On some suitable **pretext** Whymper was led through the store-shed and allowed to catch a **glimpse** of the bins. He was deceived, and continued to report to the outside world that there was no food shortage on Animal Farm.

Nevertheless, towards the end of January it became obvious that it would be necessary to **procure** some more grain from somewhere. In these days Napoleon **rarely** appeared in public, but spent all his time in the farmhouse, which was guarded at each door by fierce-looking dogs. When he did **emerge**, it was in a **ceremonial** manner, with an escort of six dogs who closely surrounded him and **growled** if anyone came too near. Frequently he did not even appear on Sunday mornings, but issued his orders through one of the other pigs, usually Squealer.

One Sunday morning Squealer announced that the hens, who had just come in to lay again, must **surrender** their eggs. Napoleon had accepted, through Whymper, a **contract** for four hundred eggs a week. The price of these would pay for enough grain and meal to keep the farm going till summer came on and conditions were easier.

When the hens heard this, they raised a terrible **outcry**. They had been warned earlier that this sacrifice might be necessary, but had not believed that it would really happen. They were just getting their **clutches** ready for the spring **sitting**, and they protested that to take the eggs away now was murder. For the first time since the expulsion of Jones, there was something resembling a rebellion. Led by three young Black Minorca **pullets**, the hens made a determined effort to **thwart** Napoleon's wishes. Their method was to fly up to the rafters and there lay their eggs, which smashed to

---

emerge [imə́:rdʒ] v.
나오다, 나타나다
ceremonial [sèrəmóuniəl] adj.
의식의, 의례상의, 격식을 차린
growl [graul] v.
으르렁거리다

surrender [səréndər] v.
내어 주다, 넘겨 주다
contract [kántrækt / kɔ́n-] n.
계약, 약정

outcry [áutkrài] n.
절규, 외침
clutch [klʌtʃ] n.
한 번에 품는 알; 한 배에 깐 병아리
sitting [sítiŋ] n.
알 품기, 포란(抱卵)
pullet [púlit] n.
(한 살 이하의) 어린 암탉
thwart [θwɔ:rt] v.
훼방놓다, 방해하다

ruthlessly [rú:əlisli] adv.
무정하게, 무자비하게
decree [dikrí:] v.
(법령에 의거하여) 명하다, 선언하다
see to it:
주의깊게 돌보다, 확실히 하다
carry out:
실행하다, 수행하다
hold out:
계속 견디다, 저항하다
capitulate [kəpítʃəlèit] v.
항복하다
give out:
알리다, 발표하다
coccidiosis [kɑksidousis] n.
(가축, 새 등의) 콕시디움증

term [tə:rm] n.
사이, 관계
spinney [spíni] n.
덤불, 잡목숲
make up one's mind:
결심하다, 결론을 내리다

pieces on the floor. Napoleon acted swiftly and **ruthlessly**. He ordered the hens' rations to be stopped, and **decreed** that any animal giving so much as a grain of corn to a hen should be punished by death. The dogs **saw to it** that these orders were **carried out**. For five days the hens **held out**, then they **capitulated** and went back to their nesting boxes. Nine hens had died in the meantime. Their bodies were buried in the orchard, and it was **given out** that they had died of **coccidiosis**. Whymper heard nothing of this affair, and the eggs were duly delivered, a grocer's van driving up to the farm once a week to take them away.

All this while no more had been seen of Snowball. He was rumoured to be hiding on one of the neighbouring farms, either Foxwood or Pinchfield. Napoleon was by this time on slightly better **terms** with the other farmers than before. It happened that there was in the yard a pile of timber which had been stacked there ten years earlier when a beech **spinney** was cleared. It was well seasoned, and Whymper had advised Napoleon to sell it; both Mr. Pilkington and Mr. Frederick were anxious to buy it. Napoleon was hesitating between the two, unable to **make up his mind**. It was noticed that whenever he seemed on the point of coming to an agreement with Frederick, Snowball

Chapter VII

was declared to be in hiding at Foxwood, while, when he inclined towards Pilkington, Snowball was said to be at Pinchfield.

Suddenly, early in the spring, an alarming thing was discovered. Snowball was secretly **frequenting** the farm by night! The animals were so disturbed that they could hardly sleep in their stalls. Every night, it was said, he came creeping in under cover of darkness and performed all kinds of **mischief**. He stole the corn, he upset the milk-pails, he broke the eggs, he trampled the seed-beds, he gnawed the bark off the fruit trees. Whenever anything went wrong it became usual to **attribute** it to Snowball. If a window was broken or a drain was blocked up, someone was certain to say that Snowball had come in the night and done it, and when the key of the store-shed was lost, the whole farm was convinced that Snowball had thrown it down the well. Curiously enough, they went on believing this even after the mislaid key was found under a sack of meal. The cows declared **unanimously** that Snowball crept into their stalls and milked them in their sleep. The rats, which had been troublesome that winter, were also said to be **in league with** Snowball.

Napoleon decreed that there should be a full **investigation** into Snowball's activities.

---

frequent [frikwént, fríːkwənt] v. 종종 방문하다, 늘 출입하다
mischief [místʃif] n. 손해, 위해, 재해
attribute [ətríbjuːt] v. ~에 기인한다고 생각하다, ~의 결과라고 생각하다
unanimously [juːnǽnəməsli] adv. 같은 의견으로, 만장일치로
in league with: ~와 동맹하여, 결탁하여, 공모하여

investigation [invèstəgéiʃən] n. 조사, 심사

snuff [snʌf] v.
코로 들이쉬다, 냄새를 맡다
snout [snaut] n.
(돼지, 개 등의) 튀어나온 입과 코; 주둥이
sniff [snif] n.
코를 킁킁 거리기; 킁킁 냄새 맡기
distinctly [distíŋktli] adv.
명백하게, 뚜렷하게
bloodcurdling [blʌ́dkə̀:rdliŋ] adj. 소름이 끼치는, 등골이 오싹하는
growl [graul] n.
으르렁거림, 으르렁 소리

pervade [pərvéid] v.
온통 퍼지다, 고루 미치다
menace [ménəs] v.
위협하다, 위태롭게 하다

"Snowball! He has been here! I can smell him distinctly!"

With his dogs in attendance he set out and made a careful tour of inspection of the farm buildings, the other animals following at a respectful distance. At every few steps Napoleon stopped and **snuffed** the ground for traces of Snowball's footsteps, which, he said, he could detect by the smell. He snuffed in every corner, in the barn, in the cowshed, in the hen-houses, in the vegetable garden, and found traces of Snowball almost everywhere. He would put his **snout** to the ground, give several deep **sniffs**, and exclaim in a terrible voice, "Snowball! He has been here! I can smell him **distinctly**!" and at the word "Snowball" all the dogs let out **blood-curdling growls** and showed their side teeth.

The animals were thoroughly frightened. It seemed to them as though Snowball were some kind of invisible influence, **pervading** the air about them and **menacing** them with all kinds of dangers. In the evening Squealer called them together, and with an alarmed expression on his face told them that he had some serious news to report.

"Comrades!" cried Squealer, making little nervous skips, "a most terrible thing has been discovered. Snowball has sold himself to Frederick of Pinchfield Farm, who is even now plotting to attack us and take our farm away from us! Snowball is to act as his guide when the attack begins. But there is worse than that. We had thought that Snowball's rebellion was caused simply by his vanity and ambition. But we were wrong, comrades. Do you know what the real reason was? Snowball was in league with Jones from the very start! He was Jones's **secret agent** all the time. It has all been proved by documents which he left behind him and which we have only just discovered. To my mind this explains a great deal, comrades. Did we not see for ourselves how he attempted—fortunately without success—to get us defeated and destroyed at the Battle of the Cowshed?"

The animals were **stupefied**. This was a wickedness far **outdoing** Snowball's destruction of the windmill. But it was some minutes before they could fully **take** it **in**. They all remembered, or thought they remembered, how they had seen Snowball **charging** ahead of them at the Battle of the Cowshed, how he had **rallied** and encouraged them at every turn, and how he had not paused for an instant even when the pellets from Jones's gun had wounded his back. At first it was a little difficult to see how this **fitted in** with his being on Jones's side. Even Boxer, who seldom asked questions, was puzzled. He lay down, tucked his fore hoofs beneath him, shut his eyes, and with a hard effort man-

formulate [fɔ́:rmjəlèit] v.
명확히 나타내다, 공식화하다

lure [luər] v.
유혹하다, 꾀어내다
doom [du:m] n.
파멸, 멸망

arrangement [əréindʒmənt] n.
예정, 계획
graze [greiz] v.
스치다, 스치고 지나가다

aged to **formulate** his thoughts.

"I do not believe that," he said. "Snowball fought bravely at the Battle of the Cowshed. I saw him myself. Did we not give him 'Animal Hero, First Class, immediately afterwards?"

"That was our mistake, comrade. For we know now—it is all written down in the secret documents that we have found—that in reality he was trying to **lure** us to our **doom**."

"But he was wounded," said Boxer. "We all saw him running with blood."

"That was part of the **arrangement**!" cried Squealer. "Jones's shot only **grazed** him. I could show you this in his own writing, if you were able to read it. The plot was for Snowball, at the critical moment, to give the signal for flight and leave the field to the enemy. And he very nearly succeeded—I will even say, comrades, he *would* have succeeded if it had not been for our heroic Leader, Comrade Napoleon. Do you not remember how, just at the moment when Jones and his men had got inside the yard, Snowball suddenly turned and fled, and many animals followed him? And do you not remember, too, that it was just at that moment, when panic was spreading and all seemed lost, that Comrade Napoleon sprang forward with a cry of 'Death to Humanity!' and sank his teeth in Jones's leg? Surely you remember *that*, comrades?" exclaimed Squealer, **frisking** from side to side.

Now when Squealer described the scene so **graphically**, it seemed to the animals that they did remember it. At any rate, they remembered that at the critical moment of the battle Snowball had turned to flee. But Boxer was still a little uneasy.

"I do not believe that Snowball was a **traitor** at the beginning," he said finally. "What he has done since is different. But I believe that at the Battle of the Cowshed he was a good comrade."

"Our Leader, Comrade Napoleon," announced Squealer, speaking very slowly and firmly, "has stated **categorically**—categorically, comrade—that Snowball was Jones's **agent** from the very beginning-yes, and from long before the Rebellion was ever thought of."

"Ah, that is different!" said Boxer. "If Comrade Napoleon says it, it must be right."

"That is the true **spirit**, comrade!" cried Squealer, but it was noticed he cast a very ugly look at Boxer with his little twinkling eyes. He turned to go, then paused and added **impressively**: "I warn every animal on this farm to keep his eyes very wide open. For we have reason to think that some of Snowball's secret agents are **lurking** among us at this moment!"

Four days later, in the late afternoon,

---

frisk [frisk] v.
깡충깡충 뛰다, 까불며 놀다
graphically [grǽfikəli] adv.
사실적으로, 여실히, 생생하게

traitor [tréitə:r] n.
배신자, 반역자

categorically [kæ̀təgɔ́:rikəli] adv. 절대로, 단호히, 단정적으로
agent [éidʒənt] n.
정보원, 스파이

spirit [spírit] n.
기백, 기운, 용기, 충성심
impressively [imprésivli] adv.
인상적으로, 감동적으로
lurk [lə:rk] v.
숨어있다

emerge [imə́ːrdʒ] v.
나오다, 나타나다
shiver [ʃívəːr] n.
한기, 오한
cower [káuər] v.
(두렵거나 부끄러워) 움츠리다, 위축하다

survey [səːrvéi] v.
바라보다, 둘러보다
countenance [káuntənəns] n.
얼굴 표정, 안색

Napoleon ordered all the animals to assemble in the yard. When they were all gathered together, Napoleon **emerged** from the farmhouse, wearing both his medals (for he had recently awarded himself "Animal Hero, First Class," and "Animal Hero, Second Class"), with his nine huge dogs frisking round him and uttering growls that sent **shivers** down all the animals' spines. They all **cowered** silently in their places, seeming to know in advance that some terrible thing was about to happen.

Napoleon stood sternly **surveying** his audience; then he uttered a high-pitched whimper. Immediately the dogs bounded forward, seized four of the pigs by the ear and dragged them, squealing with pain and terror, to Napoleon's feet. The pigs' ears were bleeding, the dogs had tasted blood, and for a few moments they appeared to go quite mad. To the amazement of everybody, three of them flung themselves upon Boxer. Boxer saw them coming and put out his great hoof, caught a dog in mid-air, and pinned him to the ground. The dog shrieked for mercy and the other two fled with their tails between their legs. Boxer looked at Napoleon to know whether he should crush the dog to death or let it go. Napoleon appeared to change **countenance**, and sharply ordered Boxer to let the dog go, whereat Boxer lifted his hoof, and the dog slunk away, bruised and howling.

Presently the tumult died down. The four pigs waited, trembling, with guilt written on every line of their countenances. Napoleon now called upon them to confess their crimes. They were the same four pigs as had protested when Napoleon **abolished** the Sunday Meetings. Without any further prompting they confessed that they had been secretly **in touch with** Snowball ever since his **expulsion**, that they had **collaborated** with him in destroying the windmill, and that they had entered into an agreement with him to **hand over** Animal Farm to Mr. Frederick. They added that Snowball had privately admitted to them that he had been Jones's **secret agent** for years past. When they had finished their **confession**, the dogs promptly tore their throats out, and in a terrible voice Napoleon demanded whether any other animal had anything to confess.

The three hens who had been the **ringleaders** in the attempted rebellion over the eggs now came forward and stated that Snowball had appeared to them in a dream and **incited** them to **disobey** Napoleon's orders. They, too, were slaughtered. Then a goose came forward and confessed to having secreted six ears of corn during the last year's harvest and eaten

on the spot:
그 자리에서, 즉석에서
execution [èksəkjúːʃən] n.
사형 집행, 처형

in a body:
다 같이, 한 떼로
treachery [trétʃ-əri] n.
배반, 반역, 변절
retribution [rètrəbjúːʃ-ən] n.
징벌, 응보
bloodshed [blʌ́dʃèd] n.
유혈 참사, 학살
knoll [noul] n.
작은 언덕
with one accord:
하나같이, 일제히
huddle [hʌ́dl] v.
모이다

them in the night. Then a sheep confessed to having urinated in the drinking pool—urged to do this, so she said, by Snowball—and two other sheep confessed to having murdered an old ram, an especially devoted follower of Napoleon, by chasing him round and round a bonfire when he was suffering from a cough. They were all slain **on the spot**. And so the tale of confessions and **executions** went on, until there was a pile of corpses lying before Napoleon's feet and the air was heavy with the smell of blood, which had been unknown there since the expulsion of Jones.

When it was all over, the remaining animals, except for the pigs and dogs, crept away **in a body**. They were shaken and miserable. They did not know which was more shocking—the **treachery** of the animals who had leagued themselves with Snowball, or the cruel **retribution** they had just witnessed. In the old days there had often been scenes of **bloodshed** equally terrible, but it seemed to all of them that it was far worse now that it was happening among themselves. Since Jones had left the farm, until today, no animal had killed another animal. Not even a rat had been killed. They had made their way on to the little **knoll** where the half-finished windmill stood, and **with one accord** they all lay down as though **huddling** together for warmth—Clover, Muriel, Benjamin, the cows, the sheep, and a whole flock of geese and hens—everyone, indeed, except the cat, who had suddenly disappeared just before Napoleon ordered the animals to assemble. For some time nobody spoke. Only Boxer remained on his feet. He **fidgeted** to and fro, **swishing** his long black tail against his sides and occasionally uttering a little **whinny** of surprise. Finally he said:

"I do not understand it. I would not have believed that such things could happen on our farm. It must be **due to** some fault in ourselves. The solution, as I see it, is to work harder. From now onwards I shall get up a full hour earlier in the mornings."

And he moved off at his **lumbering trot** and made for the quarry. Having got there, he collected two successive loads of stone and dragged them down to the windmill before retiring for the night.

The animals huddled about Clover, not speaking. The knoll where they were lying gave them a wide **prospect** across the countryside. Most of Animal Farm was within their view—the long pasture stretching down to the main road, the hayfield, the spinney, the drinking pool, the ploughed fields where the young wheat was thick and green, and the red roofs of the

aim [eim] v.
겨누다, 목표삼다, ~하려고 노력하다
overthrow [óuvərəròu] n.
타도, 전복
look forward to:
기대하다, 예상하다, 기다리다
brood [bru:d] n.
한 배 병아리; (동물의) 한 배 새끼
roam [roum] v.
돌아다니다, 방랑하다
disobedience [dìsəbí:diəns] n.
불복종, 반항, 위반

If she could have spoken her thoughts, it would have been to say that this was not what they had aimed at when they had set themselves years ago to work for the overthrow of the human race.

farm buildings with the smoke curling from the chimneys. It was a clear spring evening. The grass and the bursting hedges were gilded by the level rays of the sun. Never had the farm—and with a kind of surprise they remembered that it was their own farm, every inch of it their own property—appeared to the animals so desirable a place. As Clover looked down the hillside her eyes filled with tears. If she could have spoken her thoughts, it would have been to say that this was not what they had **aimed** at when they had set themselves years ago to work for the **overthrow** of the human race. These scenes of terror and slaughter were not what they had **looked forward to** on that night when old Major first stirred them to rebellion. If she herself had had any picture of the future, it had been of a society of animals set free from hunger and the whip, all equal, each working according to his capacity, the strong protecting the weak, as she had protected the lost **brood** of ducklings with her foreleg on the night of Major's speech. Instead—she did not know why—they had come to a time when no one dared speak his mind, when fierce, growling dogs **roamed** everywhere, and when you had to watch your comrades torn to pieces after confessing to shocking crimes. There was no thought of rebellion or **disobedience** in her mind. She knew that, even as things were, they were far **better off** than they had been in the days of Jones, and that before all else it was needful to prevent the return of the human beings. Whatever happened she would remain faithful, work hard, carry out the orders that were given to her, and accept the leadership of Napoleon. But still, it was not for this that she and all the other animals had hoped and toiled. It was not for this that they had built the windmill and faced the bullets of Jones's gun. Such were her thoughts, though she lacked the words to express them.

At last, feeling this to be in some way a **substitute** for the words she was unable to find, she began to sing *Beasts of England*. The other animals sitting round her took it up, and they sang it three times over—very tunefully, but slowly and mournfully, in a way they had never sung it before.

They had just finished singing it for the third time when Squealer, attended by two dogs, approached them with the air of having something important to say. He announced that, by a special **decree** of Comrade Napoleon, *Beasts of England* had been abolished. From now onwards it was forbidden to sing it.

The animals were **taken aback**.

"Why?" cried Muriel.

stiffly [stif] adv.
딱딱하게, 완고하게
longing [lɔ́(:)ŋiŋ, láŋ-] n.
동경, 갈망, 열망
purpose [pə́:rpəs] n.
목적, 의도, 용도

"But that society has now been established. Clearly this song has no longer any purpose."

compose [kəmpóuz] v.
만들다, 작문하다, 작곡하다

come up to:
~에 필적하다, ~만큼 좋다

"It is no longer needed, comrade," said Squealer **stiffly**. "*Beasts of England* was the song of the Rebellion. But the Rebellion is now completed. The execution of the traitors this afternoon was the final act. The enemy both external and internal has been defeated. In *Beasts of England* we expressed our **longing** for a better society in days to come. But that society has now been established. Clearly this song has no longer any **purpose**."

Frightened though they were, some of the animals might possibly have protested, but at this moment the sheep set up their usual bleating of "Four legs good, two legs bad," which went on for several minutes and put an end to the discussion.

So *Beasts of England* was heard no more. In its place Minimus, the poet, had **composed** another song which began:

Animal Farm , Animal Farm ,
Never through me shalt thou come to harm!

and this was sung every Sunday morning after the hoisting of the flag. But somehow neither the words nor the tune ever seemed to the animals to **come up to** *Beasts of England*.

Chapter VIII

hearing [híəriŋ] n.
신문, 심리; 청문회
take place:
발생하다, 일어나다
square [skwɛə:r] v.
맞다, 적합하다, 일치하다
meddle [médl] v.
참견하다, 간섭하다
fetch [fetʃ] v.
가져오다, 데려오다
somehow or other:
이럭저럭, 어떻게든지 하여

A few days later, when the terror caused by the executions had died down, some of the animals remembered—or thought they remembered—that the Sixth Commandment decreed "No animal shall kill any other animal." And though no one cared to mention it in the **hearing** of the pigs or the dogs, it was felt that the killings which had **taken place** did not **square** with this. Clover asked Benjamin to read her the Sixth Commandment, and when Benjamin, as usual, said that he refused to **meddle** in such matters, she **fetched** Muriel. Muriel read the Commandment for her. It ran: "No animal shall kill any other animal *without cause*." **Somehow or other**, the last two words had slipped out of the animals' memory. But they saw now that the Commandment had not been **violated**; for clearly there was good reason for killing the traitors who had **leagued** themselves with Snowball.

Throughout the year the animals worked even harder than they had worked in the previous year. To rebuild the windmill, with walls twice as thick as before, and to finish it by the appointed date, together with the regular work of the farm, was a tremendous labour. There were times when it seemed to the animals that they worked longer hours and fed no better than they had done in Jones's day. On Sunday mornings Squealer, holding down a long strip of paper with his trotter, would read out to them lists of figures proving that the production of every class of foodstuff had increased by two hundred per cent, three hundred per cent, or five hundred per cent, as the case might be. The animals saw no reason to **disbelieve** him, especially as they could no longer remember very clearly what conditions had been like before the Rebellion. All the same, there were days when they felt that they **would sooner** have had less figures and more food.

All orders were now issued through Squealer or one of the other pigs. Napoleon himself was not seen in public as often as once in a

fortnight [fɔ́:rtnàit] n.
2주간
retinue [rét-ənjùː] n.
(특히 왕, 귀족의) 수행원, 종자(從者)들
trumpeter [trʌ́mpitə:r] n.
나팔수, 큰 소리로 알리는 사람
inhabit [inhǽbit] v.
살다, 거주하다
wait on:
모시다, 시중을 들다
drawing room:
응접실

refer [rifə́:r] v.
~라고 부르다, 말하다
ignorance [ígnərəns] n.
무식, 무지, 모름
slavery [sléivəri] n.
노예 상태, 노예의 신분
stroke [strouk] n.
(갑작스런) 우연한 발생, 돌발

fortnight. When he did appear, he was attended not only by his **retinue** of dogs but by a black cockerel who marched in front of him and acted as a kind of **trumpeter**, letting out a loud "cock-a-doodle-doo" before Napoleon spoke. Even in the farmhouse, it was said, Napoleon **inhabited** separate apartments from the others. He took his meals alone, with two dogs to **wait upon** him, and always ate from the Crown Derby dinner service which had been in the glass cupboard in the **drawing room**. It was also announced that the gun would be fired every year on Napoleon's birthday, as well as on the other two anniversaries.

Napoleon was now never spoken of simply as "Napoleon." He was always **referred** to in formal style as "our Leader, Comrade Napoleon," and the pigs liked to invent for him such titles as Father of All Animals, Terror of Mankind, Protector of the Sheep-fold, Ducklings' Friend, and the like. In his speeches. Squealer would talk with the tears rolling down his cheeks of Napoleon's wisdom, the goodness of his heart, and the deep love he bore to all animals everywhere, even and especially the unhappy animals who still lived in **ignorance** and **slavery** on other farms. It had become usual to give Napoleon the credit for every successful achievement and every **stroke** of good fortune. You would often hear one hen remark to another, "Under the guidance of our Leader, Comrade Napoleon, I have laid five eggs in six days"; or two cows, enjoying a drink at the pool, would exclaim, "Thanks to the leadership of Comrade Napoleon, how excellent this water tastes!" The general feeling on the farm was well expressed in a poem entitled *Comrade Napoleon*, which was composed by Minimus and which ran as follows:

Friend of the fatherless!
Fountain of happiness!
Lord of the swill-bucket! Oh, how my soul is on
Fire when I gaze at thy
Calm and **commanding** *eye,*
Like the sun in the sky,
Comrade Napoleon!

Thou art the giver of
All that thy creatures love,
Full belly twice a day, clean straw to roll upon;
Every beast great or small
Sleeps at peace in his stall,
Thou watchest over all,
Comrade Napoleon!

Had I a sucking-pig,

---

commanding [kəmǽndiŋ / -máːnd-] adj.
명령조인, 당당한, 위엄있는

Friend of the fatherless!
Fountain of happiness!
Lord of the swill-bucket! Oh, how my soul is on
Fire when I gaze at thy
Calm and commanding eye,
Like the sun in the sky,
Comrade Napoleon!

ere [ɛər] prep. conj.
before
rolling pin:
(반죽을 미는) 밀방망이
squeak [skwi:k] n.
빽빽 우는 소리

surmount [sərmáunt] v.
~의 위에 놓다, ~에 얹히다
profile [próufail] n.
옆얼굴

negotiation [nigòuʃiéiʃən] n.
협상, 교섭, 절충
skulk [skʌlk] v.
슬그머니 숨다, 살금살금 하다
precaution [prikɔ́:ʃən] n.
조심, 경계

Ere he had grown as big
*Even as a pint bottle or as a **rolling-pin**,*
He should have learned to be
Faithful and true to thee,
*Yes, his first **squeak** should be*
"Comrade Napoleon!"

Napoleon approved of this poem and caused it to be inscribed on the wall of the big barn, at the opposite end from the Seven Commandments. It was **surmounted** by a portrait of Napoleon, in **profile**, executed by Squealer in white paint.

Meanwhile, through the agency of Whymper, Napoleon was engaged in complicated **negotiations** with Frederick and Pilkington. The pile of timber was still unsold. Of the two, Frederick was the more anxious to get hold of it, but he would not offer a reasonable price. At the same time there were renewed rumours that Frederick and his men were plotting to attack Animal Farm and to destroy the windmill, the building of which had aroused furious jealousy in him. Snowball was known to be still **skulking** on Pinchfield Farm. In the middle of the summer the animals were alarmed to hear that three hens had come forward and confessed that, inspired by Snowball, they had entered into a plot to murder Napoleon. They were executed immediately, and fresh **precautions**

lest [lest] conj.
~하지 않을까(라는)

give out:
알리다, 발표하다
distrust [distrʌ́st] v.
믿지 않다, 의심하다, 의아스럽게 여기다
wear on:
(시간이) 천천히 흐르다
impending [impéndiŋ] adj.
임박한, 곧 일어날 듯한
treacherous [trétʃ-ərəs] adj.
배반하는, 믿을 수 없는
bribe [braib] v.
뇌물을 주다
magistrate [mǽdʒəstrèit, -trit] n. 법관, 판사, 행정관
title deed:
(부동산) 권리증서
leak [li:k] v.
새어나오다, (비밀 등이) 누설되다

for Napoleon's safety were taken. Four dogs guarded his bed at night, one at each corner, and a young pig named Pinkeye was given the task of tasting all his food before he ate it, **lest** it should be poisoned.

At about the same time it was **given out** that Napoleon had arranged to sell the pile of timber to Mr. Pilkington; he was also going to enter into a regular agreement for the exchange of certain products between Animal Farm and Foxwood. The relations between Napoleon and Pilkington, though they were only conducted through Whymper, were now almost friendly. The animals **distrusted** Pilkington, as a human being, but greatly preferred him to Frederick, whom they both feared and hated. As the summer **wore on**, and the windmill neared completion, the rumours of an **impending treacherous** attack grew stronger and stronger. Frederick, it was said, intended to bring against them twenty men all armed with guns, and he had already **bribed** the **magistrates** and police, so that if he could once get hold of the **title deeds** of Animal Farm they would ask no questions. Moreover, terrible stories were **leaking** out from Pinchfield about the cruelties that Frederick practised upon his animals. He had flogged an old horse to death, he starved his cows, he had killed a dog by throwing it into

spur [spə:r] n.
(새의) 며느리 발톱
clamor [klǽmər] v.
외치다, 시끄럽게 요구하다
in a body:
다 같이, 한 떼로
rash [ræʃ] adj.
무모한, 성급한

dignity [dígnəti] n.
위엄, 존엄성, 품위, 긍지
scoundrel [skáundr-əl] n.
무뢰한, 악당
tiding [taidiŋ] n.
소식, 정보, 뉴스
machination [mæ̀kənéiʃ-ən] n.
책동, 간계, 음모
lay bare:
폭로하다, 털어놓다
seed corn:
종자용 옥수수
gander [gǽndər] n.
거위의 수컷
privy [prívi] adj.
내밀히 관여하는

the furnace, he amused himself in the evenings by making cocks fight with splinters of razor-blade tied to their **spurs**. The animals' blood boiled with rage when they heard of these things being done to their comrades, and sometimes they **clamoured** to be allowed to go out **in a body** and attack Pinchfield Farm, drive out the humans, and set the animals free. But Squealer counselled them to avoid **rash** actions and trust in Comrade Napoleon's strategy.

Nevertheless, feeling against Frederick continued to run high. One Sunday morning Napoleon appeared in the barn and explained that he had never at any time contemplated selling the pile of timber to Frederick; he considered it beneath his **dignity**, he said, to have dealings with **scoundrels** of that description. The pigeons who were still sent out to spread **tidings** of the Rebellion were forbidden to set foot anywhere on Foxwood, and were also ordered to drop their former slogan of "Death to Humanity" in favour of "Death to Frederick." In the late summer yet another of Snowball's **machinations** was **laid bare**. The wheat crop was full of weeds, and it was discovered that on one of his nocturnal visits Snowball had mixed weed seeds with the **seed corn**. A **gander** who had been **privy** to the plot had confessed his guilt to Squealer and

far from:
~하기는 커녕, 결코 ~아니다
censure [sénʃər] v.
비난하다, 나무라다, 견책하다
cowardice [káuərdis] n.
겁, 소심, 비겁
bewilderment [biwíldərmənt] n. 당황, 어리둥절함
at fault:
잘못하여, 착각하여, 혼동되어

in the teeth of:
~을 무릅쓰고, ~에 반대하여
punctually [pʌ́ŋktʃuəli] adv.
제시간에, 어김없이
masterpiece [mǽstə:rpì:s, mɑ́:s-] n.
걸작, 명작
explosive [iksplóusiv] n.
폭약, 폭발물

immediately committed suicide by swallowing deadly nightshade berries. The animals now also learned that Snowball had never—as many of them had believed hitherto—received the order of "Animal Hero, First Class." This was merely a legend which had been spread some time after the Battle of the Cowshed by Snowball himself. So **far from** being decorated, he had been **censured** for showing **cowardice** in the battle. Once again some of the animals heard this with a certain **bewilderment**, but Squealer was soon able to convince them that their memories had been **at fault**.

In the autumn, by a tremendous, exhausting effort—for the harvest had to be gathered at almost the same time—the windmill was finished. The machinery had still to be installed, and Whymper was negotiating the purchase of it, but the structure was completed. **In the teeth of** every difficulty, in spite of inexperience, of primitive implements, of bad luck and of Snowball's treachery, the work had been finished **punctually** to the very day! Tired out but proud, the animals walked round and round their **masterpiece**, which appeared even more beautiful in their eyes than when it had been built the first time. Moreover, the walls were twice as thick as before. Nothing short of **explosives** would lay them low this time! And when they thought of how they had laboured, what **discouragements** they had overcome, and the enormous difference that would be made in their lives when the sails were turning and the dynamos running—when they thought of all this, their tiredness **forsook** them and they **gambolled** round and round the windmill, uttering cries of triumph. Napoleon himself, attended by his dogs and his cockerel, came down to inspect the completed work; he personally congratulated the animals on their achievement, and announced that the mill would be named Napoleon Mill.

Two days later the animals were called together for a special meeting in the barn. They were struck dumb with surprise when Napoleon announced that he had sold the pile of timber to Frederick. Tomorrow Frederick's wagons would arrive and begin **carting** it away. Throughout the whole period of his seeming friendship with Pilkington, Napoleon had really been in secret agreement with Frederick.

All relations with Foxwood had been broken off; insulting messages had been sent to Pilkington. The pigeons had been told to avoid Pinchfield Farm and to alter their slogan from "Death to Frederick" to "Death to Pilkington." At the same time Napoleon assured the animals that the stories of an **impending** attack on

exaggerate [igzǽdʒərèit] v.
과장하다, 침소봉대하다
agent [éidʒənt] n.
정보원, 스파이
pensioner [pénʃənər] n.
연금 수령자

Animal Farm were completely untrue, and that the tales about Frederick's cruelty to his own animals had been greatly **exaggerated**. All these rumours had probably originated with Snowball and his **agents**. It now appeared that Snowball was not, after all, hiding on Pinchfield Farm, and in fact had never been there in his life: he was living—in considerable luxury, so it was said—at Foxwood, and had in reality been a **pensioner** of Pilkington for years past.

The pigs were in ecstasies over Napoleon's cunning. By seeming to be friendly with Pilkington he had forced Frederick to raise his price by twelve pounds. But the superior quality of Napoleon's mind, said Squealer, was shown in the fact that he trusted nobody, not even Frederick. Frederick had wanted to pay for the timber with something called a cheque, which, it seemed, was a piece of paper with a promise to pay written upon it. But Napoleon was too clever for him. He had demanded payment in real five-pound notes, which were to be handed over before the timber was removed. Already Frederick had paid up; and the sum he had paid was just enough to buy the machinery for the windmill.

Meanwhile the timber was being carted away at high speed. When it was all gone, another special meeting was held in the barn for the

beatifically [bìːətífikəli] adv.
기뻐서, 행복에 넘쳐
flimsy [flímzi] adj.
무른, 약한, 얄팍한

hullabaloo [hʌ́ləbəlùː] n.
왁자지껄, 떠들썩, 큰 소란
forgery [fɔ́ːrdʒəri] n.
모조품, 위조
for nothing:
무료로, 거저

sentinel [séntənəl] n.
보초병, 파수꾼

animals to inspect Frederick's bank-notes. Smiling **beatifically**, and wearing both his decorations, Napoleon reposed on a bed of straw on the platform, with the money at his side, neatly piled on a china dish from the farmhouse kitchen. The animals filed slowly past, and each gazed his fill. And Boxer put out his nose to sniff at the bank-notes, and the **flimsy** white things stirred and rustled in his breath.

Three days later there was a terrible **hullabaloo**. Whymper, his face deadly pale, came racing up the path on his bicycle, flung it down in the yard and rushed straight into the farmhouse. The next moment a choking roar of rage sounded from Napoleon's apartments. The news of what had happened sped round the farm like wildfire. The bank-notes were **forgeries**! Frederick had got the timber **for nothing**!

Napoleon called the animals together immediately and in a terrible voice pronounced the death sentence upon Frederick. When captured, he said, Frederick should be boiled alive. At the same time he warned them that after this treacherous deed the worst was to be expected. Frederick and his men might make their long-expected attack at any moment. **Sentinels** were placed at all the approaches to the farm. In addition, four pigeons were sent to Foxwood

conciliatory [kənsíliətò:ri / -təri] adj.
달래는, 회유적인, 타협적인

lookout [lúkàut] n.
망보는 사람, 감시인
sally [sǽli] v.
출격하다
pellet [pélit] n.
탄알, 산탄
rally [rǽli] v.
다시 모으다, 불러 모으다, 집중시키다
chink [tʃiŋk] n.
갈라진 틈, 틈새
knothole [nɑthoul / nɔthoul] n.
옹이구멍
at a loss:
난처하여, 당황하여, 어찌할 바를 몰라
wistful [wístfəl] adj.
탐나는 듯한, 동경하는 듯한

with a **conciliatory** message, which it was hoped might reestablish good relations with Pilkington.

The very next morning the attack came. The animals were at breakfast when the **look-outs** came racing in with the news that Frederick and his followers had already come through the five-barred gate. Boldly enough the animals **sallied** forth to meet them, but this time they did not have the easy victory that they had had in the Battle of the Cowshed. There were fifteen men, with half a dozen guns between them, and they opened fire as soon as they got within fifty yards. The animals could not face the terrible explosions and the stinging **pellets**, and in spite of the efforts of Napoleon and Boxer to **rally** them, they were soon driven back. A number of them were already wounded. They took refuge in the farm buildings and peeped cautiously out from **chinks** and **knotholes**. The whole of the big pasture, including the windmill, was in the hands of the enemy. For the moment even Napoleon seemed **at a loss**. He paced up and down without a word, his tail rigid and twitching. **Wistful** glances were sent in the direction of Foxwood. If Pilkington and his men would help them, the day might yet be won. But at this moment the four pigeons, who had been sent out on the day before, returned, one of them bearing a scrap of paper from Pilkington. On it was pencilled the words: "**Serves you right**."

Meanwhile Frederick and his men had halted about the windmill. The animals watched them, and a **murmur** of **dismay** went round. Two of the men had produced a **crowbar** and a **sledge hammer**. They were going to knock the windmill down.

"Impossible!" cried Napoleon. "We have built the walls far too thick for that. They could not knock it down in a week. Courage, comrades!"

But Benjamin was watching the movements of the men intently. The two with the hammer and the crowbar were drilling a hole near the base of the windmill. Slowly, and with an air almost of amusement, Benjamin nodded his long muzzle.

"I thought so," he said. "Do you not see what they are doing? In another moment they are going to pack **blasting powder** into that hole."

Terrified, the animals waited. It was impossible now to venture out of the shelter of the buildings. After a few minutes the men were seen to be running in all directions. Then there was a deafening roar. The pigeons swirled into the air, and all the animals, except Napoleon, flung themselves flat on their bellies and hid their faces. When they got up again, a huge

drown [draun] v.
압도하다, 지우다
vile [vail] adj.
몹시 나쁜, 불쾌한, 사악한
contemptible [kəntémptəbəl] adj. 멸시할 만한, 경멸할 만한, 비열한
heed [hi:d] v.
주의하다, 조심하다
hail [heil] n.
싸락눈, 우박
close quarters:
비좁은 장소; 접근전, 백병전
unscathed [ʌnskéiðd] adj.
다치지 않은, 상처를 입지 않은
detour [díːtuər, ditúər] n.
우회로, 에움길
bay [bei] v.
짖다, 으르렁거리다

cloud of black smoke was hanging where the windmill had been. Slowly the breeze drifted it away. The windmill had ceased to exist!

At this sight the animals' courage returned to them. The fear and despair they had felt a moment earlier were **drowned** in their rage against this **vile**, **contemptible** act. A mighty cry for vengeance went up, and without waiting for further orders they charged forth in a body and made straight for the enemy. This time they did not **heed** the cruel pellets that swept over them like **hail**. It was a savage, bitter battle. The men fired again and again, and, when the animals got to **close quarters**, lashed out with their sticks and their heavy boots. A cow, three sheep, and two geese were killed, and nearly everyone was wounded. Even Napoleon, who was directing operations from the rear, had the tip of his tail chipped by a pellet. But the men did not go **unscathed** either. Three of them had their heads broken by blows from Boxer's hoofs; another was gored in the belly by a cow's horn; another had his trousers nearly torn off by Jessie and Bluebell. And when the nine dogs of Napoleon's own body-guard, whom he had instructed to make a **detour** under cover of the hedge, suddenly appeared on the men's flank, **baying** ferociously, panic overtook them. They saw that they were in danger of being surrounded. Frederick shouted to his men to get out while the going was good, and the next moment the **cowardly** enemy was running for dear life. The animals chased them right down to the bottom of the field, and got in some last kicks at them as they forced their way through the thorn hedge.

They had won, but they were weary and bleeding. Slowly they began to limp back towards the farm. The sight of their dead comrades stretched upon the grass moved some of them to tears. And for a little while they halted in sorrowful silence at the place where the windmill had once stood. Yes, it was gone; almost the last trace of their labour was gone! Even the foundations were partially destroyed. And in rebuilding it they could not this time, as before, make use of the fallen stones. This time the stones had vanished too. The force of the explosion had flung them to distances of hundreds of yards. It was as though the windmill had never been.

As they approached the farm Squealer, who had **unaccountably** been absent during the fighting, came skipping towards them, **whisking** his tail and beaming with satisfaction. And the animals heard, from the direction of the farm buildings, the solemn booming of a gun.

"What is that gun firing for?" said Boxer.

occupation [ὰkjəpéiʃən / ɔ́k-] n.
점유, 거주, 점령

brace [breis] v.
긴장하다, 대비하다, 마음을 다잡다
occur [əkə́:r] v.
(문득) 생각나다

"To celebrate our victory!" cried Squealer.

"What victory?" said Boxer. His knees were bleeding, he had lost a shoe and split his hoof, and a dozen pellets had lodged themselves in his hind leg.

"What victory, comrade? Have we not driven the enemy off our soil—the sacred soil of Animal Farm?"

"But they have destroyed the windmill. And we had worked on it for two years!"

"What matter? We will build another windmill. We will build six windmills if we feel like it. You do not appreciate, comrade, the mighty thing that we have done. The enemy was in **occupation** of this very ground that we stand upon. And now—thanks to the leadership of Comrade Napoleon—we have won every inch of it back again!"

"Then we have won back what we had before," said Boxer.

"That is our victory," said Squealer.

They limped into the yard. The pellets under the skin of Boxer's leg smarted painfully. He saw ahead of him the heavy labour of rebuilding the windmill from the foundations, and already in imagination he **braced** himself for the task. But for the first time it **occurred** to him that he was eleven years old and that perhaps his great muscles were not quite what they had once been.

But when the animals saw the green flag flying, and heard the gun firing again—seven times it was fired in all—and heard the speech that Napoleon made, congratulating them on their conduct, it did seem to them after all that they had won a great victory. The animals slain in the battle were given a solemn funeral. Boxer and Clover pulled the wagon which served as a **hearse**, and Napoleon himself walked at the head of the **procession**. Two whole days were given over to celebrations. There were songs, speeches, and more firing of the gun, and a special gift of an apple was **bestowed** on every animal, with two ounces of corn for each bird and three biscuits for each dog. It was announced that the battle would be called the Battle of the Windmill, and that Napoleon had created a new decoration, the Order of the Green Banner, which he had **conferred** upon himself. In the general rejoicings the unfortunate affair of the bank-notes was forgotten.

It was a few days later than this that the pigs came upon a case of whisky in the cellars of the farmhouse. It had been **overlooked** at the time when the house was first occupied. That night there came from the farmhouse the sound of loud singing, in which, to everyone's surprise, the **strains** of *Beasts of England* were

dejectedly [didʒéktidli] adv.
기운 없이, 낙담하여
impart [impá:rt] v.
전하다, 알리다

lamentation [læməntéiʃ-ən, -men-] n.
슬퍼함, 한탄, 비탄
contrive [kəntráiv] v.
꾀하다, 획책하다, 도모하다
pronounce [prənáuns] v.
단언하다, 언명하다, 공언하다
decree [dikrí:] n.
법령, 포고, 명령

mixed up. At about half-past nine Napoleon, wearing an old bowler hat of Mr. Jones's, was distinctly seen to emerge from the back door, gallop rapidly round the yard, and disappear indoors again. But in the morning a deep silence hung over the farmhouse. Not a pig appeared to be stirring. It was nearly nine o'clock when Squealer made his appearance, walking slowly and **dejectedly**, his eyes dull, his tail hanging limply behind him, and with every appearance of being seriously ill. He called the animals together and told them that he had a terrible piece of news to **impart**. Comrade Napoleon was dying!

A cry of **lamentation** went up. Straw was laid down outside the doors of the farmhouse, and the animals walked on tiptoe. With tears in their eyes they asked one another what they should do if their Leader were taken away from them. A rumour went round that Snowball had after all **contrived** to introduce poison into Napoleon's food. At eleven o'clock Squealer came out to make another announcement. As his last act upon earth, Comrade Napoleon had **pronounced** a solemn **decree**: the drinking of alcohol was to be punished by death.

By the evening, however, Napoleon appeared to be somewhat better, and the following morning Squealer was able to tell them that he was

paddock [pǽdək] n.
방목장
set aside:
(돈이나 물건 등을) 따로 떼어 놓다, 모아두다

incident [ínsədənt] n.
사건, 생긴 일
crash [kræʃ] n.
갑자기 나는 요란한 소리, 충돌
sprawl [sprɔ:l] v.
큰대자로 드러눕다, 손발을 쭉 뻗다

..., and near at hand there lay a lantern, a paint-brush, and an overturned pot of white paint.

well on the way to recovery. By the evening of that day Napoleon was back at work, and on the next day it was learned that he had instructed Whymper to purchase in Willingdon some booklets on brewing and distilling. A week later Napoleon gave orders that the small **paddock** beyond the orchard, which it had previously been intended to **set aside** as a grazing-ground for animals who were past work, was to be ploughed up. It was given out that the pasture was exhausted and needed re-seeding; but it soon became known that Napoleon intended to sow it with barley.

About this time there occurred a strange **incident** which hardly anyone was able to understand. One night at about twelve o'clock there was a loud **crash** in the yard, and the animals rushed out of their stalls. It was a moonlit night. At the foot of the end wall of the big barn, where the Seven Commandments were written, there lay a ladder broken in two pieces. Squealer, temporarily stunned, was **sprawling** beside it, and near at hand there lay a lantern, a paint-brush, and an overturned pot of white paint. The dogs immediately made a ring round Squealer, and escorted him back to the farmhouse as soon as he was able to walk. None of the animals could form any idea as to what this meant, except old Benjamin,

knowing [nóuiŋ] adj.
알고 있는, 무언가 아는 듯한

to excess:
과도하게, 지나치게

who nodded his muzzle with a **knowing** air, and seemed to understand, but would say nothing.

But a few days later Muriel, reading over the Seven Commandments to herself, noticed that there was yet another of them which the animals had remembered wrong. They had thought that the Fifth Commandment was "No animal shall drink alcohol," but there were two words that they had forgotten. Actually the Commandment read: "No animal shall drink alcohol *to excess*."

Chapter IX

hoof [hu:f, huf] n.
발굽; (발굽을 가진 동물의) 발
a point of honor:
명예에 관한 일, 체면에 관한 일
poultice [póultis] n.
찜질약; 습포

Boxer's split **hoof** was a long time in healing. They had started the rebuilding of the windmill the day after the victory celebrations were ended. Boxer refused to take even a day off work, and made it **a point of honour** not to let it be seen that he was in pain. In the evenings he would admit privately to Clover that the hoof troubled him a great deal. Clover treated the hoof with **poultices** of herbs which she prepared by chewing them, and both she and Benjamin urged Boxer to work less hard. "A horse's lungs do not last for ever," she said to him. But Boxer would not listen. He had, he said, only one real ambition left—to see the windmill well under way before he reached

formulate [fɔ́:rmjəlèit] v.
형식으로 나타내다, 공식화하다
liberal [líb-ərəl] adj.
관대한, 아끼지 않는, 풍부한
pension [pénʃən] n.
연금
of late:
요즘, 최근에
superannuated [sù:pəræn-juèitid] adj.
노령으로 퇴직한, 연금을 받고 퇴직한

equality [i(:)kwáləti / -kwɔ́l-] n.
같음, 대등, 평등
contrary [kántreri / kɔ́n-] adv.
반대로, ~에 반하여

the age for retirement.

At the beginning, when the laws of Animal Farm were first **formulated**, the retiring age had been fixed for horses and pigs at twelve, for cows at fourteen, for dogs at nine, for sheep at seven, and for hens and geese at five. **Liberal** old-age **pensions** had been agreed upon. As yet no animal had actually retired on pension, but **of late** the subject had been discussed more and more. Now that the small field beyond the orchard had been set aside for barley, it was rumoured that a corner of the large pasture was to be fenced off and turned into a grazing-ground for **superannuated** animals. For a horse, it was said, the pension would be five pounds of corn a day and, in winter, fifteen pounds of hay, with a carrot or possibly an apple on public holidays. Boxer's twelfth birthday was due in the late summer of the following year.

Meanwhile life was hard. The winter was as cold as the last one had been, and food was even shorter. Once again all rations were reduced, except those of the pigs and the dogs. A too rigid **equality** in rations, Squealer explained, would have been **contrary** to the principles of Animalism. In any case he had no difficulty in proving to the other animals that they were *not* in reality short of food, whatever the appearances might be. For the time being, certainly, it had been found necessary to make a **readjustment** of rations (Squealer always spoke of it as a "readjustment," never as a "reduction"), but in comparison with the days of Jones, the improvement was enormous. Reading out the figures in a shrill, rapid voice, he proved to them in detail that they had more oats, more hay, more turnips than they had had in Jones's day, that they worked shorter hours, that their drinking water was of better quality, that they lived longer, that a larger **proportion** of their young ones survived infancy, and that they had more straw in their stalls and suffered less from fleas. The animals believed every word of it. Truth to tell, Jones and all he stood for had almost **faded** out of their memories. They knew that life nowadays was harsh and bare, that they were often hungry and often cold, and that they were usually working when they were not asleep. But doubtless it had been worse in the old days. They were glad to believe so. Besides, in those days they had been slaves and now they were free, and that made all the difference, as Squealer did not fail to point out.

There were many more mouths to feed now. In the autumn the four **sows** had all **littered** about simultaneously, producing thirty-one

---

readjustment [rì:ədʒʌ́stmənt] n. 재조정
proportion [prəpɔ́:rʃən] n. 비, 비율, 몫, 할당
fade [feid] v. 흐릿해지다, 희미해지다, 어렴풋해지다

sow [sau] n. 암퇘지; (곰 따위의) 암컷
litter [lítər] v. (돼지 따위가 새끼를) 낳다

piebald [páibɔ̀:ld] adj.
흑백 얼룩의
parentage [pɛ́ərəntidʒ] n.
어버이임, 부모와 자식의 관계
stand aside:
비켜서다
privilege [prívəlidʒ] n.
특권, 특전

forbid [fəːrbíd] v.
금하다, 허락하지 않다

young pigs between them. The young pigs were **piebald**, and as Napoleon was the only boar on the farm, it was possible to guess at their **parentage**. It was announced that later, when bricks and timber had been purchased, a schoolroom would be built in the farmhouse garden. For the time being, the young pigs were given their instruction by Napoleon himself in the farmhouse kitchen. They took their exercise in the garden, and were discouraged from playing with the other young animals. About this time, too, it was laid down as a rule that when a pig and any other animal met on the path, the other animal must **stand aside**: and also that all pigs, of whatever degree, were to have the **privilege** of wearing green ribbons on their tails on Sundays.

The farm had had a fairly successful year, but was still short of money. There were the bricks, sand, and lime for the schoolroom to be purchased, and it would also be necessary to begin saving up again for the machinery for the windmill. Then there were lamp oil and candles for the house, sugar for Napoleon's own table (he **forbade** this to the other pigs, on the ground that it made them fat), and all the usual replacements such as tools, nails, string, coal, wire, scrap-iron, and dog biscuits. A stump of hay and part of the potato crop

contract [kɑ́ntrækt / kɔ́n-] n.
계약, 약정
appetizing [ǽpitàiziŋ] adj.
식욕을 돋우는, 구미가 당기게 하는
waft [wɑ:ft, wæft] v.
떠돌다, 부유하다
disuse [disjú:z] v.
사용하지 않다, 폐기하다
mash [mæʃ] n.
곡식알, 밀기울 등을 더운 물에 걸쭉하게 푼 가축 사료
tureen [tjurí:n] n.
뚜껑 달린 움푹한 그릇

offset [ɔ̀:fsét, àf-] v.
상쇄하다, 맞비기다, 벌충하다

were sold off, and the **contract** for eggs was increased to six hundred a week, so that that year the hens barely hatched enough chicks to keep their numbers at the same level. Rations, reduced in December, were reduced again in February, and lanterns in the stalls were forbidden to save oil. But the pigs seemed comfortable enough, and in fact were putting on weight if anything. One afternoon in late February a warm, rich, **appetising** scent, such as the animals had never smelt before, **wafted** itself across the yard from the little brew-house, which had been **disused** in Jones's time, and which stood beyond the kitchen. Someone said it was the smell of cooking barley. The animals sniffed the air hungrily and wondered whether a warm **mash** was being prepared for their supper. But no warm mash appeared, and on the following Sunday it was announced that from now onwards all barley would be reserved for the pigs. The field beyond the orchard had already been sown with barley. And the news soon leaked out that every pig was now receiving a ration of a pint of beer daily, with half a gallon for Napoleon himself, which was always served to him in the Crown Derby soup **tureen**.

But if there were hardships to be borne, they were partly **offset** by the fact that life

dignity [dígnəti] n.
위엄, 존엄성, 품위, 긍지
precinct [príːsiŋkt] n.
경내, 영역, 주변
recitation [rèsətéiʃ-ən] n.
낭독, 암송
on occasion:
이따금, 때때로
devotee [dèvoutíː] n.
헌신하는 사람, 열성가

And the news soon leaked out that every pig was now receiving a ration of a pint of beer daily, with half a gallon for Napoleon himself, ...

nowadays had a greater **dignity** than it had had before. There were more songs, more speeches, more processions. Napoleon had commanded that once a week there should be held something called a Spontaneous Demonstration, the object of which was to celebrate the struggles and triumphs of Animal Farm. At the appointed time the animals would leave their work and march round the **precincts** of the farm in military formation, with the pigs leading, then the horses, then the cows, then the sheep, and then the poultry. The dogs flanked the procession and at the head of all marched Napoleon's black cockerel. Boxer and Clover always carried between them a green banner marked with the hoof and the horn and the caption, 'Long live Comrade Napoleon!" Afterwards there were **recitations** of poems composed in Napoleon's honour, and a speech by Squealer giving particulars of the latest increases in the production of foodstuffs, and **on occasion** a shot was fired from the gun. The sheep were the greatest **devotees** of the Spontaneous Demonstration, and if anyone complained (as a few animals sometimes did, when no pigs or dogs were near) that they wasted time and meant a lot of standing about in the cold, the sheep were sure to silence him with a tremendous bleating of "Four legs good, two legs bad!" But **by and large** the animals enjoyed these celebrations. They found it comforting to be reminded that, after all, they were truly their own masters and that the work they did was for their own benefit. So that, **what with** the songs, the processions, Squealer's lists of figures, the thunder of the gun, the crowing of the cockerel, and the fluttering of the flag, they were able to forget that their bellies were empty, at least part of the time.

In April, Animal Farm was proclaimed a Republic, and it became necessary to **elect** a President. There was only one **candidate**, Napoleon, who was elected **unanimously**. On the same day it was given out that fresh documents had been discovered which revealed further details about Snowball's **complicity** with Jones. It now appeared that Snowball had not, as the animals had previously imagined, merely attempted to lose the Battle of the Cowshed by means of a **stratagem**, but had been openly fighting on Jones's side. In fact, it was he who had actually been the leader of the human forces, and had charged into battle with the words "Long live Humanity!" on his lips. The wounds on Snowball's back, which a few of the animals still remembered to have seen, had been inflicted by Napoleon's teeth.

In the middle of the summer Moses the raven

flap [flæp] v.
퍼덕거리다, 펄럭이게 하다
contemptuously
[kəntémptʃuəsli] adv.
얕보듯이, 경멸하듯이
gill [ʤil] n.
질(액량의 단위, 1/4 pint)

apart from:
~은 제쳐 놓고, 별도로 하고

suddenly reappeared on the farm, after an absence of several years. He was quite unchanged, still did no work, and talked in the same strain as ever about Sugarcandy Mountain. He would perch on a stump, **flap** his black wings, and talk by the hour to anyone who would listen. "Up there, comrades," he would say solemnly, pointing to the sky with his large beak—"up there, just on the other side of that dark cloud that you can see—there it lies, Sugarcandy Mountain, that happy country where we poor animals shall rest for ever from our labours!" He even claimed to have been there on one of his higher flights, and to have seen the everlasting fields of clover and the linseed cake and lump sugar growing on the hedges. Many of the animals believed him. Their lives now, they reasoned, were hungry and laborious; was it not right and just that a better world should exist somewhere else? A thing that was difficult to determine was the attitude of the pigs towards Moses. They all declared **contemptuously** that his stories about Sugarcandy Mountain were lies, and yet they allowed him to remain on the farm, not working, with an allowance of a **gill** of beer a day.

After his hoof had healed up, Boxer worked harder than ever. Indeed, all the animals worked like slaves that year. **Apart from** the

insufficient [insəfíʃənt] adj.
불충분한, 부족한
falter [fɔ́ːltər] v.
비틀거리다, 주저하다
hide [haid] n.
가축의 가죽
haunch [hɔːntʃ, hɑːntʃ] n.
둔부, 허리
pick up:
좋아지다, 나아지다, 증가하다
so long as:
~하는 한, ~이기만 하다면

regular work of the farm, and the rebuilding of the windmill, there was the schoolhouse for the young pigs, which was started in March. Sometimes the long hours on **insufficient** food were hard to bear, but Boxer never **faltered**. In nothing that he said or did was there any sign that his strength was not what it had been. It was only his appearance that was a little altered; his **hide** was less shiny than it had used to be, and his great **haunches** seemed to have shrunken. The others said, "Boxer will **pick up** when the spring grass comes on"; but the spring came and Boxer grew no fatter. Sometimes on the slope leading to the top of the quarry, when he braced his muscles against the weight of some vast boulder, it seemed that nothing kept him on his feet except the will to continue. At such times his lips were seen to form the words, "I will work harder"; he had no voice left. Once again Clover and Benjamin warned him to take care of his health, but Boxer paid no attention. His twelfth birthday was approaching. He did not care what happened **so long as** a good store of stone was accumulated before he went on pension.

Late one evening in the summer, a sudden rumour ran round the farm that something had happened to Boxer. He had gone out alone to drag a load of stone down to the windmill.

And sure enough, the rumour was true. A few minutes later two pigeons came racing in with the news: "Boxer has fallen! He is lying on his side and can't get up!"

About half the animals on the farm rushed out to the knoll where the windmill stood. There lay Boxer, between the shafts of the cart, his neck stretched out, unable even to raise his head. His eyes were glazed, his sides matted with sweat. A thin stream of blood had trickled out of his mouth. Clover dropped to her knees at his side.

"Boxer!" she cried, "how are you?"

"It is my lung," said Boxer in a weak voice. "It does not matter. I think you will be able to finish the windmill without me. There is a pretty good store of stone accumulated. I had only another month to go **in any case**. To tell you the truth, I had been **looking forward to** my retirement. And perhaps, as Benjamin is growing old too, they will let him retire at the same time and be a companion to me."

"We must get help at once," said Clover. "Run, somebody, and tell Squealer what has happened."

All the other animals immediately raced back to the farmhouse to give Squealer the news. Only Clover remained, and Benjamin, who lay down at Boxer's side, and, without

---

in any case:
어떤 일이 있어도, 여하튼
look forward to:
기대하다, 예상하다, 기다리다

distress [distrés] n.
고뇌, 비탄
misfortune [misfɔ́:rtʃən] n.
불운, 불행
veterinary [vétərənèri / -rinəri] adj.
가축병 치료의, 수의학의
satisfactorily [sæ̀tisfǽktərəli] adv. 만족하게, 마음껏, 더할 나위 없이

profess [prəfés] v.
공언하다, 단언하다

speaking, kept the flies off him with his long tail. After about a quarter of an hour Squealer appeared, full of sympathy and concern. He said that Comrade Napoleon had learned with the very deepest **distress** of this **misfortune** to one of the most loyal workers on the farm, and was already making arrangements to send Boxer to be treated in the hospital at Willingdon. The animals felt a little uneasy at this. Except for Mollie and Snowball, no other animal had ever left the farm, and they did not like to think of their sick comrade' in the hands of human beings. However, Squealer easily convinced them that the **veterinary** surgeon in Willingdon could treat Boxer's case more **satisfactorily** than could be done on the farm. And about half an hour later, when Boxer had somewhat recovered, he was with difficulty got on to his feet, and managed to limp back to his stall, where Clover and Benjamin had prepared a good bed of straw for him.

For the next two days Boxer remained in his stall. The pigs had sent out a large bottle of pink medicine which they had found in the medicine chest in the bathroom, and Clover administered it to Boxer twice a day after meals. In the evenings she lay in his stall and talked to him, while Benjamin kept the flies off him. Boxer **professed** not to be sorry for what had

recovery [rikʌ́v-əri] n.
회복, 복구, 쾌유

supervision [sù:pərvíʒən] n.
관리, 감독, 지휘
gallop [gǽləp] v.
질주하다, 빠르게 뛰다
bray [brei] v.
울다, 소리 높이 울다

happened. If he made a good **recovery**, he might expect to live another three years, and he looked forward to the peaceful days that he would spend in the corner of the big pasture. It would be the first time that he had had leisure to study and improve his mind. He intended, he said, to devote the rest of his life to learning the remaining twenty-two letters of the alphabet.

However, Benjamin and Clover could only be with Boxer after working hours, and it was in the middle of the day when the van came to take him away. The animals were all at work weeding turnips under the **supervision** of a pig, when they were astonished to see Benjamin come **galloping** from the direction of the farm buildings, **braying** at the top of his voice. It was the first time that they had ever seen Benjamin excited—indeed, it was the first time that anyone had ever seen him gallop. "Quick, quick!" he shouted. "Come at once! They're taking Boxer away!" Without waiting for orders from the pig, the animals broke off work and raced back to the farm buildings. Sure enough, there in the yard was a large closed van, drawn by two horses, with lettering on its side and a sly-looking man in a low-crowned bowler hat sitting on the driver's seat. And Boxer's stall was empty.

The animals crowded round the van. "Good-bye, Boxer!" they **chorused**, "good-bye!"

"Fools! Fools!" shouted Benjamin, **prancing** round them and stamping the earth with his small hoofs. "Fools! Do you not see what is written on the side of that van?"

That gave the animals pause, and there was a **hush**. Muriel began to spell out the words. But Benjamin pushed her aside and in the midst of a deadly silence he read:

" 'Alfred Simmonds, Horse Slaughterer and Glue Boiler, Willingdon. Dealer in Hides and Bone-Meal. Kennels Supplied.' Do you not understand what that means? They are taking Boxer to the knacker's!"

A cry of horror burst from all the animals. At this moment the man on the box whipped up his horses and the van moved out of the yard at a smart trot. All the animals followed, crying out at the tops of their voices. Clover forced her way to the front. The van began to gather speed. Clover tried to stir her stout limbs to a gallop, and achieved a **canter**. "Boxer!" she cried. "Boxer! Boxer! Boxer!" And just at this moment, as though he had heard the **uproar** outside. Boxer's face, with the white stripe down his nose, appeared at the small window at the back of the van.

"Boxer!" cried Clover in a terrible voice.

matchwood [mǽtʃwùd] n.
성냥개비 재료; 산산조각
desperation [dèspəréiʃən] n.
절망, 자포자기
brute [bru:t] n.
짐승

"Boxer! Get out! Get out quickly! They are taking you to your death!"

All the animals took up the cry of "Get out, Boxer, get out!" But the van was already gathering speed and drawing away from them. It was uncertain whether Boxer had understood what Clover had said. But a moment later his face disappeared from the window and there was the sound of a tremendous drumming of hoofs inside the van. He was trying to kick his way out. The time had been when a few kicks from Boxer's hoofs would have smashed the van to **matchwood**. But alas! his strength had left him; and in a few moments the sound of drumming hoofs grew fainter and died away. In **desperation** the animals began appealing to the two horses which drew the van to stop. "Comrades, comrades!" they shouted. "Don't take your own brother to his death!" But the stupid **brutes**, too ignorant to realise what was happening, merely set back their ears and quickened their pace. Boxer's face did not reappear at the window. Too late, someone thought of racing ahead and shutting the five-barred gate; but in another moment the van was through it and rapidly disappearing down the road. Boxer was never seen again.

Three days later it was announced that he had died in the hospital at Willingdon, **in spite**

in spite of:
~에도 불구하고

of receiving every attention a horse could have. Squealer came to announce the news to the others. He had, he said, been present during Boxer's last hours.

"It was the most **affecting** sight I have ever seen!" said Squealer, lifting his trotter and wiping away a tear. "I was at his bedside at the very last. And at the end, almost too weak to speak, he whispered in my ear that his sole sorrow was to have **passed on** before the windmill was finished. 'Forward, comrades!' he whispered. 'Forward **in the name of** the Rebellion. Long live Animal Farm! Long live Comrade Napoleon! Napoleon is always right.' Those were his very last words, comrades."

Here Squealer's **demeanour** suddenly changed. He fell silent for a moment, and his little eyes darted **suspicious glances** from side to side before he proceeded.

It had come to his knowledge, he said, that a foolish and wicked rumour had been circulated at the time of Boxer's removal. Some of the animals had noticed that the van which took Boxer away was marked "Horse Slaughterer," and had actually **jumped to the conclusion** that Boxer was being sent to the knacker's. It was almost unbelievable, said Squealer, that any animal could be so stupid. Surely, he cried **indignantly**, whisking his tail

paint out:
(페인트, 물감 등으로) 칠해서 지우다

relieve [rilíːv] v.
(고통, 부탁, 걱정 따위를) 경감하다, 덜다, 해방하다
graphic [grǽfik] adj.
사실적인, 생생한
temper [témpəːr] v.
부드럽게 하다, 진정시키다

oration [ɔːréiʃən] n.
연설
interment [intə́ːrmənt] n.
매장
wreath [riːθ] n.
화관, 화환
laurel [lɔ́ːrəl, lɑ́ːr-] n.
월계수, 월계관
banquet [bǽŋkwit] n.
연회, 향연
reminder [rimáindəːr] n.
생각나게 하는 사람이나 물건

and skipping from side to side, surely they knew their beloved Leader, Comrade Napoleon, better than that? But the explanation was really very simple. The van had previously been the property of the knacker, and had been bought by the veterinary surgeon, who had not yet **painted** the old name **out**. That was how the mistake had arisen.

The animals were enormously **relieved** to hear this. And when Squealer went on to give further **graphic** details of Boxer's death-bed, the admirable care he had received, and the expensive medicines for which Napoleon had paid without a thought as to the cost, their last doubts disappeared and the sorrow that they felt for their comrade's death was **tempered** by the thought that at least he had died happy.

Napoleon himself appeared at the meeting on the following Sunday morning and pronounced a short **oration** in Boxer's honour. It had not been possible, he said, to bring back their lamented comrade's remains for **interment** on the farm, but he had ordered a large **wreath** to be made from the **laurels** in the farmhouse garden and sent down to be placed on Boxer's grave. And in a few days' time the pigs intended to hold a memorial **banquet** in Boxer's honour. Napoleon ended his speech with a **reminder** of Boxer's two favourite maxims, "I will work harder" and "Comrade Napoleon is always right"—maxims, he said, which every animal would do well to adopt as his own.

On the day appointed for the banquet, a grocer's van drove up from Willingdon and delivered a large wooden **crate** at the farmhouse. That night there was the sound of **uproarious** singing, which was followed by what sounded like a violent quarrel and ended at about eleven o'clock with a tremendous crash of glass. No one stirred in the farmhouse before noon on the following day, and the word went round that from somewhere or other the pigs had acquired the money to buy themselves another case of whisky.

---

crate [kreit] n.
틀상자, 나무 상자
uproarious [ʌpróːriəs] adj.
소란스러운, 시끄러운, 몹시 우스운

Napoleon ended his speech with a reminder of Boxer's two favourite maxims, "I will work harder" and "Comrade Napoleon is always right"

Chapter X

flee [fliː] v.
지나가다, 사라지다

Years passed. The seasons came and went, the short animal lives **fled** by. A time came when there was no one who remembered the old days before the Rebellion, except Clover, Benjamin, Moses the raven, and a number of the pigs.

rheumy [rúːmi] adj.
(눈, 코 등이) 점액을 분비하는

Muriel was dead; Bluebell, Jessie, and Pincher were dead. Jones too was dead—he had died in an inebriates' home in another part of the county. Snowball was forgotten. Boxer was forgotten, except by the few who had known him. Clover was an old stout mare now, stiff in the joints and with a tendency to **rheumy** eyes. She was two years past the retiring age, but in fact no animal had ever

superannuated [sù:pərǽn-juèitid] adj.
노령으로 퇴직한, 연금을 받고 퇴직한
morose [məróus] adj.
시무룩한, 까다로운
taciturn [tǽsətə̀:rn] adj.
말이 없는

filial [fíliəl] adj.
자식의, 자식다운

actually retired. The talk of setting aside a corner of the pasture for **superannuated** animals had long since been dropped. Napoleon was now a mature boar of twenty-four stone. Squealer was so fat that he could with difficulty see out of his eyes. Only old Benjamin was much the same as ever, except for being a little greyer about the muzzle, and, since Boxer's death, more **morose** and **taciturn** than ever.

There were many more creatures on the farm now, though the increase was not so great as had been expected in earlier years. Many animals had been born to whom the Rebellion was only a dim tradition, passed on by word of mouth, and others had been bought who had never heard mention of such a thing before their arrival. The farm possessed three horses now besides Clover. They were fine upstanding beasts, willing workers and good comrades, but very stupid. None of them proved able to learn the alphabet beyond the letter B. They accepted everything that they were told about the Rebellion and the principles of Animalism, especially from Clover, for whom they had an almost **filial** respect; but it was doubtful whether they understood very much of it.

The farm was more prosperous now, and better organised: it had even been enlarged by two fields which had been bought from Mr.

denounce [dináuns] v.
공공연히 비난하다, 매도하다
contrary [kántreri / kɔ́n-] adv.
반대로, ~에 반하여
frugally [frú:g-əli] adv.
검약하게, 소박하게

Pilkington. The windmill had been successfully completed at last, and the farm possessed a threshing machine and a hay elevator of its own, and various new buildings had been added to it. Whymper had bought himself a dogcart. The windmill, however, had not after all been used for generating electrical power. It was used for milling corn, and brought in a handsome money profit. The animals were hard at work building yet another windmill; when that one was finished, so it was said, the dynamos would be installed. But the luxuries of which Snowball had once taught the animals to dream, the stalls with electric light and hot and cold water, and the three-day week, were no longer talked about. Napoleon had **denounced** such ideas as **contrary** to the spirit of Animalism. The truest happiness, he said, lay in working hard and living **frugally**.

Somehow it seemed as though the farm had grown richer without making the animals themselves any richer — except, of course, for the pigs and the dogs. Perhaps this was partly because there were so many pigs and so many dogs. It was not that these creatures did not work, after their fashion. There was, as Squealer was never tired of explaining, endless work in the supervision and organisation of the farm. Much of this work was of a kind that the other

> Somehow it seemed as though the farm had grown richer without making the animals themselves any richer — except, of course, for the pigs and the dogs.

animals were too ignorant to understand. For example, Squealer told them that the pigs had to **expend** enormous labours every day upon mysterious things called "files", "reports", "**minutes**", and "memoranda. These were large sheets of paper which had to be closely covered with writing, and as soon as they were so covered, they were burnt in the furnace. This was of the highest importance for the welfare of the farm, Squealer said. But still, neither pigs nor dogs produced any food by their own labour; and there were very many of them, and their appetites were always good.

As for the others, their life, so far as they knew, was as it had always been. They were generally hungry, they slept on straw, they drank from the pool, they laboured in the fields; in winter they were troubled by the cold, and in summer by the flies. Sometimes the older ones among them **racked** their dim memories and tried to determine whether in the early days of the Rebellion, when Jones's expulsion was still recent, things had been better or worse than now. They could not remember. There was nothing with which they could compare their present lives: they had nothing to go upon except Squealer's lists of figures, which **invariably demonstrated** that everything was getting better and better. The animals found

insoluble [insάljubəl / -sɔ́l-] adj. 풀리지 않는, 해결할 수 없는
speculate [spékjəlèit] v. 숙고하다, 사색하다, 추측하다
unalterable [ʌnɔ́:ltərəbəl] adj. 변경할 수 없는, 불변의

give up: 그만두다, 포기하다, 단념하다
marvel [mά:rv-əl] v. 놀라다, 경탄하다
swell [swel] v. (감정이) 고조되다, 뿌듯해지다
imperishable [impériʃəbəl] adj. 불멸의, 불후의, 영속적인
expulsion [ikspʌ́lʃən] n. 추방, 배제, 제명
foretell [fɔ:rtél] v. 예언하다, 예고하다

the problem **insoluble**; in any case, they had little time for **speculating** on such things now. Only old Benjamin professed to remember every detail of his long life and to know that things never had been, nor ever could be much better or much worse—hunger, hardship, and disappointment being, so he said, the **unalterable** law of life.

And yet the animals never **gave up** hope. More, they never lost, even for an instant, their sense of honour and privilege in being members of Animal Farm. They were still the only farm in the whole county—in all England!—owned and operated by animals. Not one of them, not even the youngest, not even the newcomers who had been brought from farms ten or twenty miles away, ever ceased to **marvel** at that. And when they heard the gun booming and saw the green flag fluttering at the masthead, their hearts **swelled** with **imperishable** pride, and the talk turned always towards the old heroic days, the **expulsion** of Jones, the writing of the Seven Commandments, the great battles in which the human invaders had been defeated. None of the old dreams had been abandoned. The Republic of the Animals which Major had **foretold**, when the green fields of England should be untrodden by human feet, was still believed in. Some day it was coming: it might not be soon, it might not be within the lifetime of any animal now living, but still it was coming. Even the tune of *Beasts of England* was perhaps **hummed** secretly here and there: **at any rate**, it was a fact that every animal on the farm knew it, though no one would have dared to sing it aloud. It might be that their lives were hard and that not all of their hopes had been fulfilled; but they were conscious that they were not as other animals. If they went hungry, it was not from feeding **tyrannical** human beings; if they worked hard, at least they worked for themselves. No creature among them went upon two legs. No creature called any other creature "Master." All animals were equal.

One day in early summer Squealer ordered the sheep to follow him, and led them out to a piece of waste ground at the other end of the farm, which had become overgrown with **birch saplings**. The sheep spent the whole day there **browsing** at the leaves under Squealer's supervision. In the evening he returned to the farmhouse himself, but, as it was warm weather, told the sheep to stay where they were. It ended by their remaining there for a whole week, during which time the other animals saw nothing of them. Squealer was with them for the greater part of every day. He was, he said,

---

hum [hʌm] v.
콧노래를 부르다
at any rate:
하여튼, 좌우간에
tyrannical [tiránik-əl, tai-] adj.
폭군의, 전제적인, 포악한

birch [bəːrtʃ] n.
자작나무
sapling [sǽpliŋ] n.
묘목, 어린 나무
browse [brauz] v.
(풀 등을) 먹다

teaching them to sing a new song, for which privacy was needed.

It was just after the sheep had returned, on a pleasant evening when the animals had finished work and were making their way back to the farm buildings, that the terrified neighing of a horse sounded from the yard. Startled, the animals stopped in their tracks. It was Clover's voice. She **neighed** again, and all the animals broke into a gallop and rushed into the yard. Then they saw what Clover had seen.

It was a pig walking on his hind legs.

Yes, it was Squealer. A little awkwardly, as though not quite used to supporting his considerable bulk in that position, but with perfect balance, he was **strolling** across the yard. And a moment later, out from the door of the farmhouse came a long file of pigs, all walking on their hind legs. Some did it better than others, one or two were even a trifle unsteady and looked as though they would have liked the support of a stick, but every one of them made his way right round the yard successfully. And finally there was a tremendous baying of dogs and a shrill crowing from the black cockerel, and out came Napoleon himself, majestically upright, casting **haughty** glances from side to side, and with his dogs gambolling round him.

He carried a whip in his trotter.

There was a deadly silence. Amazed, terrified, **huddling** together, the animals watched the long line of pigs march slowly round the yard. It was as though the world had turned **upside-down**. Then there came a moment when the first shock had worn off and when, in spite of everything—in spite of their terror of the dogs, and of the habit, developed through long years, of never complaining, never criticising, no matter what happened—they might have uttered some word of **protest**. But just at that moment, as though at a signal, all the sheep burst out into a tremendous bleating of—

"Four legs good, two legs *better*! Four legs good, two legs *better*! Four legs good, two legs *better*!"

It went on for five minutes without stopping. And by the time the sheep had quieted down, the chance to utter any protest had passed, for the pigs had marched back into the farmhouse.

Benjamin felt a nose **nuzzling** at his shoulder. He looked round. It was Clover. Her old eyes looked dimmer than ever. Without saying anything, she tugged gently at his mane and led him round to the end of the big barn, where the Seven Commandments were written. For a minute or two they stood gazing at the tarred wall with its white lettering.

"My sight is failing," she said finally. "Even

when I was young I could not have read what was written there. But it appears to me that that wall looks different. Are the Seven Commandments the same as they used to be, Benjamin?"

For once Benjamin consented to break his rule, and he read out to her what was written on the wall. There was nothing there now except a single Commandment. It ran:

ALL ANIMALS ARE EQUAL
BUT SOME ANIMALS ARE MORE EQUAL
THAN OTHERS

After that it did not seem strange when next day the pigs who were supervising the work of the farm all carried whips in their trotters. It did not seem strange to learn that the pigs had bought themselves a wireless set, were arranging to install a telephone, and had taken out subscriptions to *John Bull*, *Tit-Bits*, and the *Daily Mirror*. It did not seem strange when Napoleon was seen strolling in the farmhouse garden with a pipe in his mouth—no, not even when the pigs took Mr. Jones's clothes out of the wardrobes and put them on, Napoleon himself appearing in a black coat, **ratcatcher breeches**, and leather **leggings**, while his favourite sow appeared in the **watered silk** dress

---

ratcatcher [ˈkætʃəːr] n.
약식 사냥복
breeches [brítʃiz] n.
반바지, 바지
leggings [léɡiŋz] n.
각반, 레깅스
watered silk:
무아르, 파문직

ALL ANIMALS ARE EQUAL
BUT SOME ANIMALS ARE
MORE EQUAL THAN OTHERS

which Mrs. Jones had been used to wear on Sundays.

A week later, in the afternoon, a number of dogcarts drove up to the farm. A **deputation** of neighbouring farmers had been invited to make a tour of inspection. They were shown all over the farm, and expressed great admiration for everything they saw, especially the windmill. The animals were **weeding** the turnip field. They worked diligently, hardly raising their faces from the ground, and not knowing whether to be more frightened of the pigs or of the human visitors.

That evening loud laughter and bursts of singing came from the farmhouse. And suddenly, at the sound of the mingled voices, the animals were stricken with curiosity. What could be happening in there, now that for the first time animals and human beings were meeting on terms of equality? **With one accord** they began to creep as quietly as possible into the farmhouse garden.

At the gate they paused, half frightened to go on, but Clover led the way in. They tiptoed up to the house, and such animals as were tall enough peered in at the dining-room window. There, round the long table, sat half a dozen farmers and half a dozen of the more **eminent** pigs, Napoleon himself occupying the seat of

toast [toust] n.
축배, 축배의 말

incumbent [inkʌ́mbənt] adj.
의무로 지워지는, 책무인

mistrust [mistrʌ́st] n.
불신, 의혹
misunderstanding [mìsʌndə:rstǽndiŋ] n.
오해, 잘못 생각함
come to an end:
멈추다, 끝내다
proprietor [prəpráiətər] n.
소유자, 경영자
hostility [hɑstíləti / hɔs-] n.
적의, 적개심, 적대 행위
misgiving [misgívin] n.
의혹, 불안
liable [láiəb-əl] adj.
자칫하면 ~하는, ~하기 쉬운

honour at the head of the table. The pigs appeared completely at ease in their chairs. The company had been enjoying a game of cards, but had broken off for the moment, evidently in order to drink a **toast**. A large jug was circulating, and the mugs were being refilled with beer. No one noticed the wondering faces of the animals that gazed in at the window.

Mr. Pilkington, of Foxwood, had stood up, his mug in his hand. In a moment, he said, he would ask the present company to drink a toast. But before doing so, there were a few words that he felt it **incumbent** upon him to say.

It was a source of great satisfaction to him, he said—and, he was sure, to all others present—to feel that a long period of **mistrust** and **misunderstanding** had now **come to an end**. There had been a time—not that he, or any of the present company, had shared such sentiments—but there had been a time when the respected **proprietors** of Animal Farm had been regarded, he would not say with **hostility**, but perhaps with a certain measure of **misgiving**, by their human neighbours. Unfortunate incidents had occurred, mistaken ideas had been current. It had been felt that the existence of a farm owned and operated by pigs was somehow abnormal and was **liable** to have an unsettling effect in the neighbourhood. Too many farmers had **assumed**, without due enquiry, that on such a farm a spirit of **licence** and **indiscipline** would **prevail**. They had been nervous about the effects upon their own animals, or even upon their human employees. But all such doubts were now **dispelled**. Today he and his friends had visited Animal Farm and inspected every inch of it with their own eyes, and what did they find? Not only the most up-to-date methods, but a discipline and an **orderliness** which should be an example to all farmers everywhere. He believed that he was right in saying that the lower animals on Animal Farm did more work and received less food than any animals in the county. Indeed, he and his fellow-visitors today had observed many features which they intended to introduce on their own farms immediately.

He would end his remarks, he said, by **emphasising** once again the friendly feelings that **subsisted**, and ought to subsist, between Animal Farm and its neighbours. Between pigs and human beings there was not, and there need not be, any **clash** of interests whatever. Their struggles and their difficulties were one. Was not the labour problem the same everywhere? Here it became **apparent** that Mr. Pilkington was about to spring some carefully prepared **witticism** on the company, but for a moment he was too overcome by amusement to be able to utter it. After much choking, during which his various chins turned purple, he managed to get it out: "If you have your lower animals to contend with," he said, "we have our lower classes!" This **bon mot** set the table in a **roar**; and Mr. Pilkington once again congratulated the pigs on the low rations, the long working hours, and the general absence of pampering which he had observed on Animal Farm.

And now, he said finally, he would ask the company to rise to their feet and make certain that their glasses were full. "Gentlemen," concluded Mr. Pilkington, "gentlemen, I give you a toast: To the **prosperity** of Animal Farm!"

There was enthusiastic cheering and stamping of feet. Napoleon was so **gratified** that he left his place and came round the table to **clink** his mug against Mr. Pilkington's before emptying it. When the cheering had died down, Napoleon, who had remained on his feet, intimated that he too had a few words to say.

Like all of Napoleon's speeches, it was short and **to the point**. He too, he said, was happy that the period of misunderstanding was at an end. For a long time there had been rumours—circulated, he had reason to think, by some **malignant** enemy—that there was something

subversive [səbvə́:rsiv] adj.
전복하는, 파괴적인
revolutionary [rèvəlúːʃ-ənèri / -nəri] adj.
혁명의, 혁명적인
title deed:
(부동산) 권리증서

promote [prəmóut] v.
진전시키다, 증진하다, 장려하다
hitherto [hìðərtú:] adv.
지금까지

subversive and even **revolutionary** in the outlook of himself and his colleagues. They had been credited with attempting to stir up rebellion among the animals on neighbouring farms. Nothing could be further from the truth! Their sole wish, now and in the past, was to live at peace and in normal business relations with their neighbours. This farm which he had the honour to control, he added, was a co-operative enterprise. The **title-deeds**, which were in his own possession, were owned by the pigs jointly.

He did not believe, he said, that any of the old suspicions still lingered, but certain changes had been made recently in the routine of the farm which should have the effect of **promoting** confidence still further. **Hitherto** the animals on the farm had had a rather foolish custom of addressing one another as "Comrade." This was to be suppressed. There had also been a very strange custom, whose origin was unknown, of marching every Sunday morning past a boar's skull which was nailed to a post in the garden. This, too, would be suppressed, and the skull had already been buried. His visitors might have observed, too, the green flag which flew from the masthead. If so, they would perhaps have noted that the white hoof and horn with which it had previously been marked had now been removed. It would be a plain green flag from now onwards.

He had only one criticism, he said, to make of Mr. Pilkington's excellent and neighbourly speech. Mr. Pilkington had referred throughout to "Animal Farm." He could not of course know—for he, Napoleon, was only now for the first time announcing it—that the name "Animal Farm" had been abolished. Henceforward the farm was to be known as "The Manor Farm"—which, he believed, was its correct and original name.

"Gentlemen," concluded Napoleon, "I will give you the same toast as before, but in a different form. Fill your glasses **to the brim**. Gentlemen, here is my toast: To the prosperity of The Manor Farm!"

There was the same **hearty** cheering as before, and the mugs were emptied to the **dregs**. But as the animals outside gazed at the scene, it seemed to them that some strange thing was happening. What was it that had altered in the faces of the pigs? Clover's old dim eyes **flitted** from one face to another. Some of them had five chins, some had four, some had three. But what was it that seemed to be melting and changing? Then, the applause having come to an end, the company took up their cards and continued the game that had been interrupted,

---

to the brim:
가득 채워

hearty [há:rti] adj.
진심의, 따뜻한
dreg [dreg] n.
찌끼, 찌꺼기, 앙금
flit [flit] v.
경쾌하게 움직이다, 재빨리 움직이다

furious [fjú-əriəs] adj.
성난, 격노한
denial [dináiəl] n.
부인, 부정, 거절

and the animals crept silently away.

But they had not gone twenty yards when they stopped short. An uproar of voices was coming from the farmhouse. They rushed back and looked through the window again. Yes, a violent quarrel was in progress. There were shoutings, bangings on the table, sharp suspicious glances, **furious denials**. The source of the trouble appeared to be that Napoleon and Mr. Pilkington had each played an ace of spades simultaneously.

Twelve voices were shouting in anger, and they were all alike. No question, now, what had happened to the faces of the pigs. The creatures outside looked from pig to man, and from man to pig, and from pig to man again; but already it was impossible to say which was which.

November 1943 - February 1944

The creatures outside looked from pig to man, and from man to pig, and from pig to man again; but already it was impossible to say which was which.